ADVANCE CYBER SECURITY

CYBER SECURITY

DR. SHIV SHAKTI SHRIVASTAVA

Made with ♥ on the Notion Press Platform
www.notionpress.com

This book is dedicated to my mentor and my friends who taught me the discipline of being a responsible person. The book is also dedicated to my students — past, present, and future. You are the object of my inspiration and motivation; you are the reason for this book

Contents

Contents

Preface

Cyber security is widely viewed as a matter of pressing national importance. Many elements of cyberspace are notoriously vulnerable to an expanding range of attacks by a spectrum of hackers, criminals, terrorists, and state actors. For example, government agencies and private-sector companies, both large and small, suffer from cyber thefts of sensitive information, cyber vandalism (e.g., defacing of websites), and denial-of-service attacks. The nation's critical infrastructure, including the electric power grid, air traffic control system, financial systems, and communication networks, depends extensively on information technology for its operation. National policymakers have become increasingly concerned that adversaries backed by considerable resources will attempt to exploit the cyber vulnerabilities in the critical infrastructure, thereby inflicting substantial harm on the nation. Numerous policy proposals have been advanced, and a number of bills have been introduced in Congress to tackle parts of the cyber security challenge. This book is designed to serve as the textbook for a semester course devoted to cyber security. It is focused on helping students acquire the skills sought in the professional workforce.

Acknowledgements

There are many people whose efforts on this book have contributed to its successful completion. I owe each a debt of gratitude and want to take this opportunity to offer my sincere thanks.

A very special thanks to my publisher, without whose continued interest and support this book would not have been possible. Senior Professor provided support and encouragement when it was most needed. Thanks also to my Marketing Manager of Publisher, whose efforts on this book have been greatly appreciated. Finally, thanks to all the other people at the publishers.

Prologue

It is the point of this book to gracefully a down-to-earth review of both the standards and practice of advanced cyber security inside the initial piece of the book, the basic issues to be tended to by a cyber security ability are investigated by giving an instructional exercise and review of security and system security innovation. The last piece of the book manages the act of cyber security: pragmatic applications that are executed and are being used to gracefully arrange cyber security the point, and therefore this book draws on a spread of controls. In this time of all-inclusive electronic availability, infections and programmers, electronic spying, and electronic misrepresentation, there's surely no time at which cyber security doesn't make a difference. Two patterns have near structure to the subject of this book of significant intrigue, to guarantee the credibility of information and messages and to monitor frameworks from organized based assaults.

Chapter-1 Introduction of Cyber Crime

Introduction of Cyber Crime, Challenges of Cyber Crime, Classifications of Cybercrimes: E-Mail Spoofing, Spamming, Internet Time Theft, Salami attack/Salami Technique.

Chapter-2 Web jacking and Cyber terrorism

Web jacking, Online Frauds, Software Piracy, Computer Network Intrusions, Password Sniffing, Identity Theft, and Cyber terrorism, Virtual Crime, Perception of cyber criminals: hackers, insurgents and extremist group etc. Web servers were hacking, session hijacking.

Chapter-3 Cyber Crime and Criminal justice

Cyber Crime and Criminal justice: Concept of Cyber Crime and the IT Act, 2000, Hacking, Teenage Web Vandals, Cyber Fraud and Cheating, Defamation, Harassment and E-mail Abuse, Other IT Act Offences, Monetary Penalties, jurisdiction and Cyber Crimes, Nature of Criminality, Strategies to tackle Cyber Crime and Trends.

Chapter-4 The Indian Evidence Act of 1872 v. Information Technology Act, 2000

The Indian Evidence Act of 1872 v. Information Technology Act, 2000: Status of Electronic Records as Evidence, Proof and Management of Electronic Records; Relevancy, Admissibility and Probative Value of E-Evidence, Proving Digital Signatures, Proof of Electronic Agreements, Proving Electronic Messages.

Chapter-5 Tools and Methods in Cybercrime

Tools and Methods in Cybercrime: Proxy Servers and Anonymizers, Password Cracking, Key loggers and Spyware, virus and worms, Trojan Horses, Backdoors, DoS and DDoS Attacks, Buffer and Overflow, Attack on Wireless Networks, Phishing: Method of Phishing, Phishing Techniques.

Chapter-6 Protect Against and Prevent

Email scams safety precautions, securing your computer from cybercrime attacks, staying safe on social media, social Media Safety precautions, exercising caution when shopping online, safely Installation of Application, prevent spyware from getting onto your computer, protect your Identity online.

1

Introduction of Cyber Crime

information technology has transformed the global economy and connected people and markets in ways beyond imagination. With information technology gaining center stage, nations across the world are experimenting with innovative ideas for economic development and inclusive growth. It has also created new vulnerabilities and opportunities for disruption. Cyber security threats emanate from a wide variety of sources and manifest themselves in disruptive activities that target individuals, businesses, national infrastructure, and governments alike. Their effects carry significant risks for public safety, the security of the nation, and the stability of the globally linked economy as a whole. The origin of a disruption, the identity of the perpetrator, or the motivation for it can be difficult to ascertain, and the act can take place virtually anywhere. These attributes facilitate the use of information technology for disruptive activities. As such, cyber security threats pose one of the most serious economic and national security challenges.

Cyber security, also referred to as information technology security, focuses on protecting computers, networks, programs, and data from unintended or unauthorized access, change, or destruction. As the IT field is grooming continuously day by day, the dependency on them increases manifold. Computer systems now include a wide variety of smart devices such as smartphones, televisions, and other portable devices which are part of the internet of things, etc. Cyber security covers technologies, processes, and practices that are designed to protect computers, networks, programs, and data from damage, attack, or unauthorized access. A security model is described by three elements (availability, integrity, and confidentiality). Privacy infringement and security vulnerability can happen due to internal users or malicious attackers.

A security model and its elements are:

1. Availability: Making sure that the computing systems, the communication channels, and the security controls function correctly.

2. Integrity: Assuring and maintaining the consistency and accuracy of data and systems.

3. Confidentiality: Preventing the disclosure of data and information to unauthorized systems and individuals.

The realization that most of the world relies on the internet should prompt us to ask ourselves:

- How much of my life is dependent on the internet?
- How much of my personal information is stored online?
- How much of my business is accessible over networks?
- How much of my customers'/friends/relative's information is accessible over networks?

Cyber Space

The term “cyber” is derived from the word “cybernetics” which means science of communication and control over machine and man. It is the virtual computer world, in which an electronic medium is used to form a global computer network to provide online sharing and communication, known as cyber space.

Cyber space is the new horizon which is controlled by machine for information and communication between human beings across the world. Therefore, crimes committed in cyber space are to be treated as cyber-crime. It allows users to perform all activities online (using internet) such as play games, knowledge sharing, conduct business, chat or communication, study and many more things.

Introduction of cyber-crime

Cyber-crime is a crime which is conducted by the use of computer, electronic devices, and network (internet) to offences against individual or group of individuals. A person, who is involved in such type of crime, called as cyber-criminal.

The motive of cyber-criminal may be:

1. To intentionally harm the reputation of the victim
2. Cause physical or mental harm
3. Loss, to the victim directly or indirectly, using Internet and mobile phones (Bluetooth/SMS/MMS)
4. Threaten a person
5. Nation’s security
6. Financial health
7. Creating and distributing virus

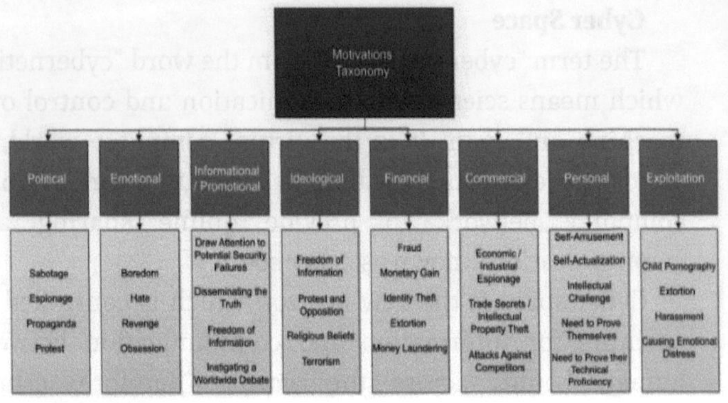

Figure 1.1: Motive of cyber-crime

Cyber Security

It is the process of protecting computers, electronic systems, networks and data from malicious attacks. Cyber security can also defend the integrity of a computer (internet connected), hardware, software, and data from various cyber-attacks. It also applies different kind of methodologies to recover networks, devices and data/ programs from any type of cyber-attack.

Figure 1.2: Cyber security applications

Importance of cyber security

1. It encompasses everything that pertains to protecting our sensitive data.
2. Protecting our financial and health information.
3. To secure personal information and intellectual property.
4. Governmental and industry information from theft and damage.
5. Also protect servers and electronic devices from various cyber-attacks.

Cyber law

Cyber law is a kind of legal system that deals with the cyber space and cyber-crime. Cyber law or IT law is a legal informatics that supervises the digital circulation of data, computer, software, and e-commerce. Cyber law is very important and essential to deals with cyber-crime.

Challenges of cyber-crime

1. Lack of awareness about cyber-crime and cyber law.
2. To implement the counter measures, there is lack of skilled and qualified manpower.
3. To join the police, the necessary eligibility should be knowledge of computer and cyber law.
4. To identify the origin of cyber-crimes and criminals, all government activities should be rapid and effective.
5. Cyber-attacks have come not only from terrorists but also from neighboring countries contrary to our national interests.
6. Promotion of Cyber Research & Development is not up to the mark.

7. Security forces and Law enforcement personnel are not equipped to address high-tech crimes.
8. Present protocols are not self-sufficient.
9. Budgets for security purpose by the government are very less from other countries.

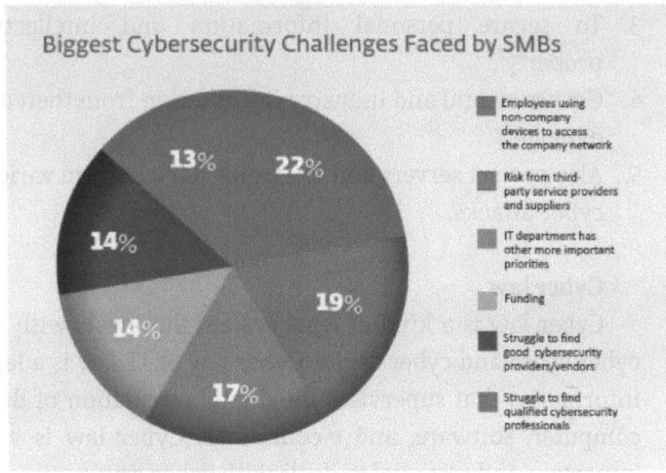

Figure 1.3: Challenges of cyber-crime faced by Small and Midsize Businesses

Difference between conventional crime and cyber crime

1. Conventional crime is as old as the human society which is focused on social and economic while cyber- crime is referring to all criminal activities done using the computers, internet, and cyber space.
2. In conventional crime, it is easy to decide jurisdiction (like in case of murder, it is easy to decide where to file a case) while in case of cyber-crime it is difficult to find jurisdiction if parties belong to different jurisdiction

(may be from different city or country).

3. In conventional crime, activities/crimes that are traditional in nature such as theft, fraud while cybercrime would be unlawful acts wherein the computer is either a tool or a target or both.
4. No specific skills required for conventional crime but for cybercrime sophisticated/technical skills required to commit crime.

Classifications of Cyber Crimes

There are many types of cyber-crime prevailing in the system; broadly we can classify them in to four major categories as discussed below:

1. **Crimes against individuals** – Some examples of cyber-crimes against individuals are:

a. Email harassment
b. Cyber-stalking
c. Spreading obscene material
d. Unauthorized access or control over the computer system
e. Indecent exposure
f. Spoofing via email
g. Fraud and also cheating
h. Further, crimes against individual property like computer vandalism and transmitting a virus.

1. **Crimes against organizations** – Some examples of cyber-crimes against organizations are:

   a. Possessing unauthorized information
   b. Cyber terrorism against a government organization

c. Distributing pirated software

1. **Crimes against society** – Some examples of crimes against society are:

a. Polluting the youth through indecent exposure
b. Trafficking
c. Financial crimes
d. Selling illegal articles
e. Online Gambling
f. Forgery

4. **Crime against property:** Another classification of cyber-crimes is, cyber-crimes against all forms of property. These crimes include computer vandalism (obliteration of others' property), intellectual property crimes, threatening, and salami attacks. This kind of crime is normally prevalent in the financial institutions or for the purpose of committing financial crimes.

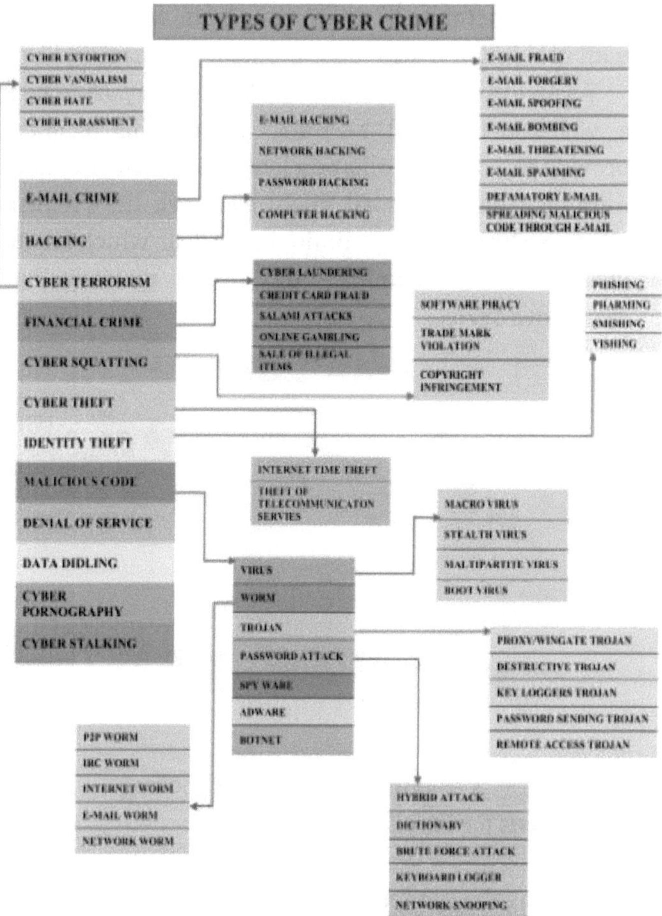

Figure 1.4: Types of cyber-crime

E-Mail spoofing

It is the deceit of an email header in the hopes of duping the recipient into thinking the email originated from someone or somewhere other than the intended source. Spoofed e-mail is one that appears to originate from one source but actually has been sent from another source. E-mail spoofing can also cause monetary damage.

As an example, a spoofed email may purport to be from a well-known retail business, asking the recipient to provide personal information like a password or credit card number. The fake email might even ask the recipient to click on a link offering a limited time deal, which is actually just a link to download and install malware on the recipient's device.

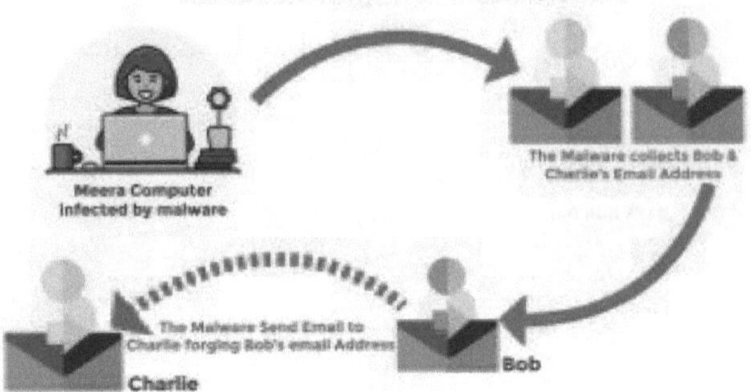

Figure 1.5: E-mail spoofing

Reasons for Email spoofing:

1. **Hiding the sender's true identity** – Though if this is the only goal, it can be achieved more easily by registering anonymous mail addresses.
2. **Avoiding spam blacklists**- If a sender is spammer, they are bound to be blacklisted quickly. A simple solution to this problem is to switch email address.
3. **Pretending to be someone the recipient knows**- In order to, for example, ask for sensitive information or access to personal assets.

4. **Pretending to be from a business the recipient has a relationship with**- As means of getting a hold of bank login details or other personal data.
5. **Tarnishing the image of the assumed sender**- A character attack that places the so-called sender in a bad light.
6. **Sending messages in someone's name can also be used to commit identity theft**- For example, by requesting information from the victim's financial or healthcare accounts.

How Emails are spoofed

The easiest way to spoof mails is for the attacker finds a mail server with an open SMTP (Simple Mail Transfer Protocol) port. SMTP lacks any authentication so servers that are poorly configured have no protection against prospective cyber criminals. It's also the case that there is nothing stopping determined attackers from setting up their own email servers. This is very common in cases of CEO/CFO fraud. Attackers will register domains easily confused for the company they are impersonating, where the email is originating from – e.g., "@exarnple.com" instead of "@example.com". Depending on the formatting of the email, it might be extremely difficult for a regular user to notice the difference.

Email spoofing protections

Since the email protocol SMTP (Simple Mail Transfer Protocol) lacks authentication, it has historically been easy to spoof a sender address. As a result, most email providers have become experts at detecting and alerting users to spam, rather than rejecting it altogether. But several frameworks have been developed to allow authentication of incoming messages.

a. **SPF (Sender Policy Framework):** This checks whether a certain IP is authorized to send mail from a given domain. SPF may lead to false positives, and still requires the receiving server to do the work of checking an SPF record, and validating the email sender.
b. **DKIM (Domain Key Identified Mail):** This method uses a pair of cryptographic keys that are used to sign outgoing messages, and validate incoming messages. However, because DKIM is only used to sign specific pieces of a message, the message can be forwarded without breaking the validity of the signature. This is technique is referred to as a "replay attack".
c. **DMARC (Domain-Based Message Authentication, Reporting, and Conformance):** This method gives a sender the option to let the receiver know whether its email is protected by SPF or DKIM, and what actions to take when dealing with mail that fails authentication. DMARC is not yet widely used.

Spamming (SPAM: stupid pointless annoying...malware?)

For the purpose of commercial advertising, non-commercial proselytizing, or for any prohibited purpose, an unsolicited message (spam) send to large numbers of recipients (especially the fraudulent purpose of phishing) by the use of messaging system is known as Spamming. E-mail spam is the well-known form of spamming.

The term spamming is also applied to other media like:

- In internet forums,
- Instant messaging,
- Mobile text messaging,
- Social networking spam,

- Junk fax transmissions,
- Television advertising and sharing network spam.

Spam advertisers have little to no operating costs and so need only a minute response rate to make a profit. The purposes of most spam are commercial advertising, but some contain viruses, adware, or scams.

How can stop spam?

- **Don't respond to spam.**
- **Turn your spam filter on.**
- **Turn macros off.**
- **Use multi-factor authentication.**

In order to deter the transmission of spamming, many e-mail providers have introduced 'spam filters' aimed at deterring the deliverance of electronic spam. Furthermore, internet browsers have undertaken methodologies utilized in order to limit, if not fully prohibit, the existence of 'pop-up solicitation', as well as the prevention of 'spyware' and additional intrusive monitoring programs. These types of preventative measures can be accessed both through paid services, as well as free services.

Internet time theft

When the internet surfing hours of the victim are used up by another person, this kind of activity called as Internet time theft. This is done by gaining access to the login ID and the password.

Internet time/bandwidth theft is a crime where the internet connection of one person (victim) is used by an unauthorized person (the criminal). This is usually done by getting access to the user's internet account details, such as user name and password, provided by the service provider.

This access can be given voluntarily by the user for a stipulated time period, or it can be gained fraudulently.

Wireless internet has made this theft more prevalent. It is easy to commit this crime if the victim uses an open WI-FI connection (one without password) for internet access.

Salami attack/salami technique

Salami slicing is a form of financial cyber-attack where the criminal takes an amount of money that is so insignificant that a single case is completely unnoticed. The amount of money taking in every case would be very little (say Rs 0.5), however the number of cases would be large. Therefore, each individual victim would incur a very small loss, but the criminal would make a sizeable amount. For example, a bank employee inserts a program into the bank's servers that takes away a very small amount (say Rs0.5) a month from every account. None of the account holders would notice this unauthorized removal of money because it is too small to notice. However due to the sheer number of accounts from which money is taken, the employee would make a sizable amount of money every month.

Real life salami attacks

A. In January 1993, four executives of a rental-car franchise in Florida were charged with defrauding at least 47,000 customers using a salami technique.
B. In Los Angeles, in October 1998, district attorneys charged four men with fraud for allegedly installing computer chips in gasoline pumps that cheated consumers by overstating the amounts pumped.
C. In 2008, a man was arrested for fraudulently creating 58,000 accounts which he used to collect money through verification deposits from online brokerage firms a few cents at a time.

D. In 1996, an Edmonton fare box serviceman was found guilty of stealing from the city's transit agency by stealing coins from the fare box. Over 13 years, he walked away with 37 tons of coins with a face value of nearly CDN$2.4 million, having used a magnet to lift the coins one at a time out of the fare boxes. He was sentenced to 4 years in prison and was eligible for parole after 18 months.

How to prevent salami attack?

1. Banks have to update their security so that the attacker doesn't familiarize himself/herself with the way the framework is designed.
2. Banks should advise customers on reporting any kind of money deduction that they aren't aware that they were a part of.
3. Whether a small or big amount, banks should encourage customers to come forward and openly tell them that this could mean that an act of fraud could very well be the scenario.
4. Most important, customers should ideally not store information online when it comes to bank details.

Difference between fraud and forgery

Fraud denotes any kind of practice of dishonesty of a person or a company for financial advantage. It is generally considered a well-thought-out crime by the law. On the other hand, forgery is essentially concerned with a produced or altered object.

Fraud is the crime of deceiving another, which may be performed through the use of objects obtained through forgery. Forgery is a common technique in fraud schemes, where the fraudster uses forged documents in order to gain access to information or materials, they should not truly have access to. Forgery is concerned with an object such as a false document, signature or a commercial good.

2

Web jacking and Cyber terrorism

Web jacking

Illegally seeking control of a website by taking over a domain is known as Web Jacking. In web jacking attack method hacker's compromises with the domain name system (DNS) that resolves website URL to IP address but the actual website is never touched.

Web jacking attack method is another type of social engineering phishing attack where an attacker create a fake web page of victim website and send it to the victim and when a victim click on that link, a message display on the browser "the site abc.com has move on another address, click here to go to the new location" and if a victim click on the link, he/she will redirect on the fake website page where an attacker can ask for any sensitive data such as credit card number, username, password etc.

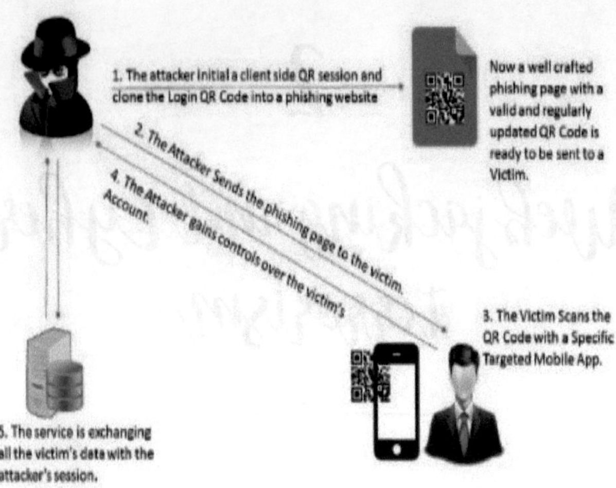

Figure 2.1: Process of web jacking

Web jacking attack method

1. The first step of web jacking attack method is to create a fake page of victim website for example www.anywebsite.com/login.php.
2. The second step is to host it either on your local computer or shared hosting.
3. The third step is to send the link of a fake page to the victim.
4. In fourth step victim will open the link and enter their details and submit.
5. In Last step attacker will get all the details submitted by victim.

How to be safe from web jacking attack method

1. First of all, do not enter sensitive data by any link sent to you.
2. Check the URL
3. Just because the address looks OK, don't assume this is a legitimate site.
4. Read company name carefully, is it right or wrong.
5. Check that there is http protocol or https, if http then do not enter your data.
6. If you are not sure about site whether it is real or fake, enter a wrong username and password.
7. Use a browser with anti-phishing detection

Online Frauds

Fraud that is committed using the internet is known as "online fraud". Online fraud can involve financial fraud and identity theft. The most common types of online fraud are called phishing and spoofing.

A. **Online Scam**-Online scam is an attempt to trap you for obtaining money. There are many types of online scams; this includes obtaining money with fake names, fake photos, fake e-mails, forged documents, fake job offers and many more.
B. **Phishing Scam**-Online scammers send you an e-mail and ask your account information or credit card details along with a link to provide your information. Generally, the links sent will be similar to your actual bank links. So whenever you post your details in the link then the details will be received and misused by scammers.
C. **Lottery Scam**-Sometimes you receive an email like "you won a lottery of million dollars". Receiving such kind of mails is a great thing, and really it's a happiest thing. By responding to such a kind of mails huge amount of

money will be lost. Because these e-Mails are not true, scammers try to fool and trap you to obtain money.

D. **Online Auction-** If you bid for a product you never get the promised product or don't match the product as shown online, and the description given to you may be incomplete, wrong, or fake.

E. **Forwarding Product or Shipping Scam-** Shipping scams are also referred to as "postal forwarding." They accept parcels (usually containing stolen items). Then they repackage and reshipping them.

F. **E-mail Scam Like- Congratulations you have won Webcam, Digital Camera, etc.-** Sometimes you get an e-mail with a message like- you have won something special like digital camera webcam, all you need to do is just visit our web site by clicking the link given below and provide your debit or credit card details to cover shipping and managing costs. However, the item never arrives but after some days the charges will be shown on your bank account and you will lose money.

Software piracy

Software piracy is the act of stealing software that is legally protected. This stealing includes copying, distributing, modifying or selling the software. Copyright laws were originally put into place so that the people who develop software (programmers, writers, graphic artists, etc.) would get the proper credit and compensation for their work. When software piracy occurs, compensation is stolen from these copyright holders.

The End-User License Agreement (EULA) is a license used for most software. It is a contract between the manufacturer and/or author and the end user. This agreement defines rules for software use and not every agreement is the same. One common rule in most EULAs prohibits users from sharing the software with others.

Types of Software Piracy

1. **Soft-lifting:** Soft-lifting is when someone purchases one version of the software and downloads it onto multiple computers, even though the software license states it should only be downloaded once. This often occurs in business or school environments and is usually done to save money. Soft-lifting is the most common type of software piracy.
2. **Client-server overuse:** Client-server overuse is when too many people on a network use one main copy of the program at the same time. This often happens when businesses are on a local area network and download the software for all employees to use. This becomes a type of software piracy if the license doesn't entitle you to use it multiple times.
3. **Hard disk loading:** Hard disk loading is a type of commercial software piracy in which someone buys a legal version of the software and then reproduces copies or installs it onto computer hard disks. The person then sells the product. This often happens at PC resale shops and buyers aren't always aware that the additional software they are buying is illegal.
4. **Counterfeiting:** Counterfeiting occurs when software programs are illegally duplicated and sold with the appearance of authenticity. Counterfeit software is usually sold at a discounted price in comparison to the legitimate software.
5. **Online Piracy:** Online piracy also known as Internet piracy is when illegal software is sold, shared or acquired by means of the Internet. This is usually done

through a peer-to-peer (P2P) file sharing system, which is usually found in the form of online auction sites and blogs.

Computer Network Intrusions

A network intrusion refers to any unauthorized activity on a digital network. Network intrusions often involve stealing valuable network resources and almost always jeopardize the security of networks and/or their data. Below are some of the most common network intrusion attack techniques:

A. **Living off the Land:** Attackers increasingly use existing tools and processes and stolen credentials when compromising networks. These tools like operating system utilities, business productivity software and scripting languages.
B. **Multi-Routing:** If a network allows for asymmetric routing, attackers will often leverage multiple routes to access the targeted device or network. This allows them to avoid being detected by having a large portion of suspicious packets bypass certain network segments and any relevant network intrusion systems.
C. **Buffer Overwriting:** By overwriting certain sections of computer memory on a network device, attackers can replace normal data in those memory locations with a slew of commands that can later be used as part of a network intrusion.
D. **Covert CGI Scripts:** Unfortunately, the Common Gateway Interface (CGI), which allows servers to pass user requests to relevant applications and receive data back to then forward to users, serves as an easy opening for attackers to access network system files.

E. **Protocol-Specific Attacks:** Protocols such as ARP, IP, TCP, UDP, ICMP, and various application protocols can inadvertently leave openings for network intrusions.

F. **Traffic Flooding:** By creating traffic loads that are too large for systems to adequately screen, attackers can induce chaos and congestion in network environments, which allows them to execute attacks without ever being detected.

G. **Trojan horse malware:** As the name suggests, Trojan Horse viruses create network backdoors that give attackers easy access to systems and any available data. Unlike other viruses and worms, Trojans don't reproduce by infecting other files, and they don't self-replicate.

H. **Worms:** One of the easiest and most damaging network intrusion techniques is the common, standalone computer virus, or worm. Often spread through email attachments or instant messaging, worms take up large amounts of network resources, preventing the authorized activity from occurring.

Intrusion Detection System (IDS)

An Intrusion Detection System (IDS) is a system that monitors network traffic for suspicious activity and issues alerts when such activity is discovered. IDS are classified into following types:

1. **Network intrusion detection system (NIDS):** Network intrusion detection systems (NIDS) are set up at a planned point within the network to examine traffic from all devices on the network.
2. **Host intrusion detection system (HIDS):** Host intrusion detection systems (HIDS) run on independent hosts or

devices on the network. A HIDS monitors the incoming and outgoing packets from the device only and will alert the administrator if suspicious or malicious activity is detected.

3. **Protocol-based intrusion detection system (PIDS):** Protocol-based intrusion detection system (PIDS) comprises of a system or agent that would consistently resides at the front end of a server, controlling and interpreting the protocol between a user/device and the server.
4. **Application protocol-based intrusion detection system (APIDS):** Application Protocol-based Intrusion Detection System (APIDS) is a system or agent that generally resides within a group of servers. It identifies the intrusions by monitoring and interpreting the communication on application specific protocols.
5. **Hybrid intrusion detection system:** Hybrid intrusion detection system is made by the combination of two or more approaches of the intrusion detection system. In the hybrid intrusion detection system, host agent or system data is combined with network information to develop a complete view of the network system.

Password sniffing

A password sniffer is a software application that scans and records passwords that are used or broadcasted on a computer or network interface. It listens to all incoming and outgoing network traffic and records any instance of a data packet that contains a password.

A password sniffer installs on a host machine and scans all incoming and outgoing network traffic. A password sniffer may be applied to most network protocols, including HTTP, Internet Message Access Protocol (IMAP), file transfer protocol (FTP), POP3, Telnet (TN) and related protocols that carry passwords in some format. In addition, a password sniffer that is installed on a gateway or proxy server can listen and retrieve all passwords that flow within a network.

There are many implementations of password sniffers, here are some examples:

- **SniffPass from NirSoft**
- **Password Sniffer Spy**
- **FTP password sniffer**
- **Sniffing Out Passwords and Cookies**
- **Ace Password Sniffer**
- **Password Sniffing with Meta-sploit**
- **Build an FTP Password Sniffer with Scapy and Python**

Identity theft

Identity theft is the crime of obtaining the personal or financial information of another person for the sole purpose of assuming that person's name or identity to make transactions or purchases. Identity theft is committed in many different ways. There are many different examples of identity theft, including:

1. **Financial identity theft:** This is the most common type of identity theft. Financial identity theft seeks economic benefits by using a stolen identity.
2. **Tax-related identity theft:** In this type of exploit, the criminal files a false tax return with the Internal Revenue Service (IRS). Done by using a stolen Social Security number.
3. **Medical identity theft:** Here, the thief steals information like health insurance number (member ID)

to receive medical services. The victim's health insurance provider may get the fraudulent bills. This will be reflected in the victim's account as services they received.

4. **Criminal identity theft:** In this exploit, a criminal gives stolen identity (other's identity) information to the police. If this type of exploit is successful, the victim is charged instead of the thief.
5. **Child identity theft:** In this exploit, a child's Social Security number is misused to apply for government benefits like opening bank accounts and other services. Children's information is often sought after by criminals because this type of damage is unnoticed for a long time.
6. **Senior identity theft:** This type of exploit targets people over the age of 60. Because senior citizens are often identified as theft targets, it is especially important for this senior to stay on top of the evolving methods thieves use to steal information.
7. **Identity cloning for concealment:** In this type of exploit, a thief impersonates someone else in order to hide from law enforcement or creditors. Because this type isn't explicitly financially motivated, it's harder to track, and there often isn't a paper trail for law enforcement to follow.
8. **Synthetic identity theft:** In this type of exploit, a thief partially or completely fabricates an identity by combining different pieces of PII (personally identifiable information) from different sources. For example, the thief may combine one stolen Social Security number with an unrelated birth date.

Cyber terrorism

Cyber terrorism is “a criminal act perpetrated by the use of computers and telecommunication capabilities resulting in violence, destruction and/or disruption of services to create fear within a given population with a goal of influencing a government or population to conform to a particular political, social or ideological agenda”.

The main aim of cyber terrorists today is to cripple critical infrastructure of a country by cyber-attacks to further the causes they espouse for as a terrorist group. In their wish lists are critical infrastructures like telecommunications, electric grids, transportation networks, banking & finance, water supply, fuel production & supply chains, military complexes, government operations and emergency services.

For Example, In the year 2000, an engineer working in Maroochy Shire Waste Water Plant, Sunshire Coast City, Australia subverted the computers of the company which controlled its operations, to vent out his feelings of frustration with the company’s promotion policies. The result was release of millions of tons of sewage water into parks and seacoast of the city causing massive environmental damage. As the act was not ideologically or politically motivated, it was not, rightly so, called an act of cyber terrorism. It was a grave cyber-crime, never the less!

Virtual crime

Virtual crime is similar to crimes that happen in real life, but in the virtual world. Virtual crime or in-game crime refers to a virtual criminal act that takes place in a massively multiplayer online game (MMOG), usually an MMORPG. The huge time and effort invested into such games can lead online "crime" to spill over into real world crime, and even blur the distinctions between the two. For example, In South Korea, where the number of computer game players is massive, some have reported the emergence of gangs and mafia, where powerful players steal and demand that beginners give them virtual money for their "protection".

Perception of cyber criminals: Hackers, insurgents and extremist group

Hackers

- Hackers and attacker's groups are any skilled computer expert that uses their technical knowledge to overcome a problem. While hacker can refer to any skilled computer programmer, the term has become associated in popular culture with a security hacker, someone who, with their technical knowledge, uses bugs or exploits to break into computer systems.
- Four primary motives have been proposed as possibilities for why hackers attempt to break into computers and networks. There is a criminal financial gain to be had when hacking systems with the specific purpose of stealing credit card numbers or manipulating banking systems.
- Many hackers thrive off of increasing their reputation within the hacker subculture and will leave their handles on websites they defaced or leave some other evidence as proof that they were involved in a specific hack.

Insurgents and extremist group

- Insurgent and extremist groups have used Internet technology as an instrument of theft in order to enhance their resource base.

Insurgents

- Interconnectedness and information technology are new aspects of this contemporary wave of insurgencies. Using the Internet, insurgents can now link virtually with allied groups throughout a state, a region, and even the entire world. Insurgents often join loose organizations with common objectives but different motivations and no central controlling body, which makes identifying leaders difficult.
- Others see the Internet as a more active weapon, enabling terrorists and insurgents to magnify the symbolic effect of their attacks. Clearly, if the 'info-sphere' is indeed an 'ungoverned space', it is one where the insurgent is determined to fight and win the 'battle for ideas.

Extremist group

- Criminals and extremists are able to take advantage of the same 'global technological commons' upon which society is becoming so dependent. Terrorists and other extremists are known to make extensive use of the Internet. The number of extremist websites has increased at an enormous rate.
- The popularity of the Internet for ideological and political extremists can be explained in a number of ways. By origin, design and function, the Internet could scarcely be improved upon as a medium for extremist organization and activity. The origins of the Internet lie in the Cold War, and in the need to ensure redundancy in governmental and military communications systems in the event of clear strike. It should be no surprise;

therefore, that extremists are also attracted to a system which offers inbuilt resilience and virtual anonymity. They may also be attracted to a system which is relatively cost-free, and where the investments necessary to develop and maintain the global communications infrastructure have already been made.

Web servers hacking

Websites are hosted on web servers. Web servers are themselves computers running an operating system; connected to the back-end database, running various applications. Web server is a system used for storing, processing, and delivering websites. It is designed to host web applications, allowing clients to access those applications.

Any vulnerability in the applications, database, operating system or in the network will lead to an attack on the web server. Just as with any computer system, web servers too can be compromised.

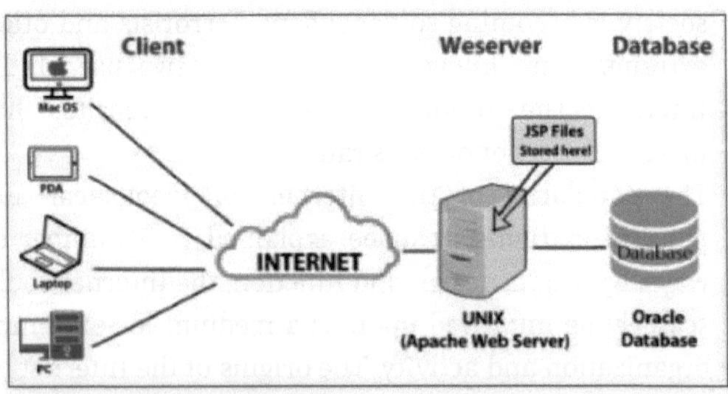

Figure 2.2: Working of web server

Attackers use various techniques to launch attacks on target web servers and gain unauthorized access. Some of the attacks include:

A. **DoS/DDoS attacks:** DoS/DDoS attack is an attack in which the attacker sends a large number of requests to the target web server to prevent the server from functioning properly. DNS Server Hijacking: DNS server hijacking attack is an attack in which the attacker targets a DNS server and tempers with its mapping settings making it redirect clients to the attacker's rogue server which serves the attacker's malicious website.
B. **Directory traversal attacks:** Directory traversal attack is an attack in which the attacker manipulates the target URL to gain access to restricted directories.
C. **MITM attacks:** Man-in-the-middle attack is an attack in which the attacker intercepts the traffic that is going from the client to the server and back. They do so by tricking the client into thinking that the attacker is a proxy. Once the client accepts the connection from the attacker, the entire communication between the client and the server goes through the attacker, allowing them to steal information.
D. **Phishing attacks:** Phishing attack is an attack in which the attacker emails the target with malicious links. Once the target clicks on the link, they are redirected to a malicious website which prompts them to provide sensitive information. The attacker then steals this information.
E. **SQL injection attacks:** Are used to deface the website. When an attacker finds out that input fields are not sanitized properly, he can add SQL strings to maliciously

craft a query which is executed by the web browser. He may store malicious/unrelated data in the database; when the website is requested, it will show irrelevant data on the website, thus displaying a defaced website.

F. **Mis-configuration attacks:** Sometimes, by mistake administrator will give access roles to the users unknowingly which permits the way such as allowing users to execute commands on the server.

G. **Phishing attack:** An attacker may redirect the victim to malicious websites by sending him/her a malicious link by email which looks authentic, but redirects him/her to malicious web page thereby stealing their data.

H. **Software bugs:** By default, the web server may have bugs and this paves a way for the attackers to gain unauthorized access to the system.

Countermeasures for web servers hacking:

1. Update and patch web servers regularly.
2. Do not use the default configuration.
3. Store configuration files securely.
4. Scan the applications running on the web server for all vulnerabilities.
5. Use IDS and firewall with updated signatures.
6. Block all unnecessary protocols and services.
7. Use secure protocols.
8. Disable default accounts, follow strict access control policy.
9. Install Anti-virus, and update it regularly.
10. All OS and software used should be latest and updated.

Session hijacking

Session hijacking is an attack where a user session is taken over by an attacker. A session starts when you log into a service, for example your banking application, and ends when you log out. The attack relies on the attacker's knowledge of your session cookie, so it is also called cookie hijacking or cookie side-jacking. Although any computer session could be hijacked, session hijacking most commonly applies to browser sessions and web applications.

In most cases when you log into a web application, the server sets a temporary session cookie in your browser to remember that you are currently logged in and authenticated. HTTP is a stateless protocol and session cookies attached to every HTTP header are the most popular way for the server to identify your browser or your current session.

To perform session hijacking, an attacker needs to know the victim's session ID (session key). This can be obtained by stealing the session cookie or persuading the user to click a malicious link containing a prepared session ID. In both cases, after the user is authenticated on the server, the attacker can take over (hijack) the session by using the same session ID for their own browser session. The server is then fooled into treating the attacker's connection as the original user's valid session. Attackers have many options for session hijacking, depending on the attack vector and the attacker's position. Some of them are:

1. **Using packet sniffers:**Using packet sniffing, attackers can monitor the user's network traffic and intercept session cookies after the user has authenticated on the server.

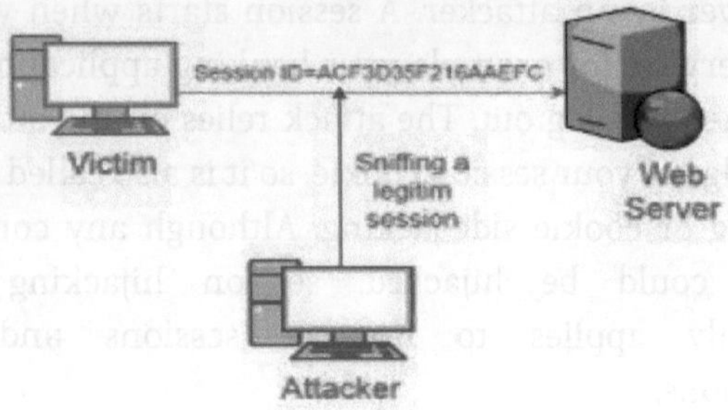

Figure 2.3: Illustration of Packet sniffing

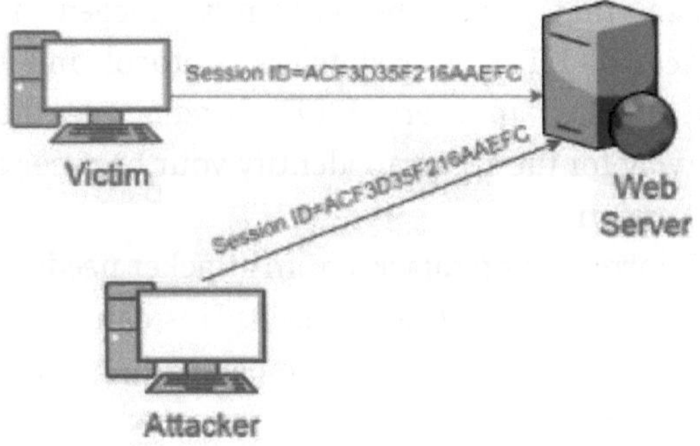

Figure 2.4: Action after Packet sniffing

2. **Cross-site scripting (XSS):** This is probably the most dangerous and widespread method of web session hijacking. By exploiting server or application vulnerabilities, attackers can inject client-side scripts (typically JavaScript) into web pages, causing your browser to execute arbitrary code when it loads a compromised page.

Figure 2.5: Illustration of session hijacking using XSS

3. Cookie theft by malware or direct access: A very common way of obtaining session cookies is to install malware on the user's machine to perform automated session sniffing.

4. Brute force: Finally, the attacker can simply try to guess the session key of a user's active session, which is feasible only if the application uses short or predictable session identifiers.

3

Cyber Crime and Criminal justice

Cyber-crime

Cyber-crime is a crime which is conducted by the use of computer, electronic devices, and network (Internet) to offences against individual or group of individuals. A person, who is involved in such type of crime, called as cyber-criminal. The motive of cyber-criminal may be:

1. To intentionally harm the reputation of the victim
2. Cause physical or mental harm
3. Loss, to the victim directly or indirectly, using Internet and mobile phones (Bluetooth/SMS/MMS)
4. Threaten a person
5. Nation's security
6. Financial health
7. Creating and distributing viruses

Cyber-crime and criminal justice

Criminal justice is the system through which crimes and criminals are identified, apprehended, judged, and punished. A criminal justice system is comprised of law, the courts, and corrections. When a crime is committed, law enforcement investigates. Once a suspect is apprehended, the courts take over. If the accused is found guilty, they are sentenced and turned over to corrections.

In the digital age, new technologies and methods of interaction with other humans and devices came into play. A cyber-crime investigator is primarily concerned with gathering evidence from digital systems that can be used in the prosecution of internet-based, or cyberspace, criminal activity. All cyber-crime includes the uses of the World Wide Web. A cyber-crime investigator can use the crucial evidences to solve cyber-crimes.

Concept of cyber-crime and the IT Act, 2000

Cyber-crime is criminal activity that either targets or uses a computer, a computer network or a networked device. Cyber-crime is committed by cybercriminals or hackers who want to make money. Cyber-crime is carried out by individuals or organizations.

Cyber law is the part of the overall legal system that deals with the internet, cyber-space, and their respective legal issues. Cyber law covers a fairly broad area covering several subtopics including freedom of expression, access to and usage of the internet, and online privacy. Cyber law is referred to as the Law of the Internet.

In 1996, the United Nations Commission on International Trade Law (UNCITRAL) adopted the model law on electronic commerce (e-commerce) to bring uniformity in the law in different countries. The Information Technology Act, 2000 or ITA, 2000 or IT Act, was notified on October 17, 2000. It is the law that deals with cyber-crime and electronic commerce in India. India became the 12th country to enable cyber law after it passed the Information Technology Act, 2000.

While the first draft was created by the Ministry of Commerce, Government of India as the E Commerce Act, 1998, it was redrafted as the 'Information Technology Bill, 1999', and passed in May 2000. Further, this act amended the Indian Penal Code 1860, the Indian Evidence Act 1872, the Bankers' Books Evidence Act 1891, and the Reserve Bank of India Act 1934.

Cyber-crimes under the IT Act

- Tampering with computer source documents - Sec.65
- Hacking with computer systems, data alteration - Sec.66
- Publishing obscene information - Sec.67
- Un-authorized access to protected system Sec.70
- Breach of confidentiality and privacy - Sec.72
- Publishing false digital signature certificates - Sec.73

Cyber-crimes under IPC and special laws

- Sending threatening messages by email - Sec 503 IPC
- Sending defamatory messages by email - Sec 499 IPC
- Forgery of electronic records - Sec 463 IPC
- Bogus websites, cyber frauds - Sec 420 IPC
- Email spoofing - Sec 463 IPC
- Web-Jacking - Sec. 383 IPC
- E-Mail abuse - Sec.500 IPC

Features of the Information Technology Act, 2000

- All electronic contracts made through secure electronic channels are legally valid.
- Legal recognition for digital signatures.
- Security measures for electronic records and also digital signatures are in place.
- A procedure for the appointment of adjudicating officers for holding inquiries under the Act is finalized
- Provision for establishing a Cyber Regulatory Appellant Tribunal under the Act. Further, this tribunal will handle all appeals made against the order of the controller or adjudicating officer.
- An appeal against the order of the Cyber Appellant Tribunal is possible only in the High Court.
- Digital signsture will use an asymmetric cryptosystem and also a hash function.
- Provision for the appointment of the Controller of Certifying Authorities (CCA) to license and regulate the working of certifying authorities.
- The Act applies to offences or contraventions committed outside India.
- Senior police officers and other officers can enter any public place and search and arrest without warrant.
- Provisions for the constitution of a Cyber Regulations Advisory Committee to advise the Central Government and Controller.

Hacking

Hacking is the act of finding the possible entry points that exist in a computer system or a computer network and finally entering into them. Hacking is usually done to gain unauthorized access to a computer system or a computer network, either to harm the systems or to steal sensitive information available on the computer. Hacking is identifying weakness in computer systems or networks to exploit its weaknesses to gain access.

Hacking is usually legal as long as it is being done to find weaknesses in a computer or network system for testing purpose. This sort of hacking is called Ethical Hacking. A computer expert who does the act of hacking is called a "Hacker".

Purpose of hacking

There could be various positive and negative intentions behind performing hacking activities. Here is a list of some probable reasons why people indulge in hacking activities –

1. Just for fun
2. Show-off
3. Steal important information
4. Damaging the system
5. Hampering privacy
6. Money extortion
7. System security testing
8. To break policy compliance.

Types of hackers

Hackers can be classified into different categories such as white hat, black hat, and grey hat, based on their intent of hacking a system.

1. **White hat hackers**

White hat hackers are also known as Ethical hackers. They never intent to harm a system, rather they try to find out weaknesses in a computer or a network system as a part of penetration testing and vulnerability assessments. Ethical hacking is not illegal and it is one of the demanding jobs available in the IT industry. There are numerous companies that hire ethical hackers for penetration testing and vulnerability assessments.

1. **Black hat hackers**

Black hat hackers, also known as crackers, are those who hack in order to gain unauthorized access to a system and harm its operations or steal sensitive information. Black hat hacking is always illegal because of its bad intent which includes stealing corporate data, violating privacy, damaging the system, blocking network communication etc.

3. **Grey hat hackers**

Grey hat hackers are a blend of both black hat and white hat hackers. They act without malicious intent but for their fun, they exploit a security weakness in a computer system or network without the owner's permission or knowledge. Their intent is to bring the weakness to the attention of the owners and getting appreciation or a little bounty from the owners.

4. **Miscellaneous hackers**

Apart from the above well-known classes of hackers, we have the following categories of hackers based on what they hack and how they do it –

A. **Red hat hackers:** Red hat hackers are again a blend of both black hat and white hat hackers. They are usually on the level of hacking government agencies, top-secret information hubs, and generally anything that falls under the category of sensitive information.

B. **Blue hat hackers: Blue hat hacker is someone outside computer security consulting firms who is used to bug-test a system prior to its launch. They look for loopholes that can be exploited and try to close these gaps. Microsoft also uses the term blue hat to represent a series of security briefing events.**
C. **Elite Hackers: This is a social status among hackers, which is used to describe the most skilled hacker. Newly discovered exploits will circulate among these hackers.**
D. **Script Kiddie: A script kiddie is a non-expert who breaks into computer systems by using pre-packaged automated tools written by others, usually with little understanding of the underlying concept, hence the term Kiddie.**
E. **Hacktivist: A hacktivist is a hacker who utilizes technology to announce a social, ideological, religious, or political message. In general, most hacktivism involves website defacement or denial-of-service attacks.**
F. **Phreaker:** A hacker who identifies and exploits weaknesses in telephones instead of computers.

Teenage web vandals

Teenage vandalism can be defining as "willful or malicious destruction, injury, disfigurement, or defacement of any public or private property, without the consent of the owner". Vandalism includes a wide variety of acts, including remove graffiti, damaging property (smashing mailboxes, trashing empty buildings or school property, breaking windows etc.), stealing street signs, eggs, cap, toilet papers, and other types of mischief.

There are a number of reasons why a teen might vandalize property

1. They could be bowing down to peer pressure.
2. Someone dared them to do it, or the girl they like admires someone else who vandalizes, or perhaps it could be part of an initiation in a gang.
3. Sometimes teens make poor decisions when they are bored. For example, a teen might view stealing a street sign as a fun way to pass time where no one gets hurt.
4. Another reason could be for revenge. A teen is angry on someone and tries to get back at that person by damaging their property.

Cyber fraud and cheating

Fraud is when trickery is used to gain a dishonest advantage, which is often financial, over another person. Here are many words used to describe fraud: scam, con, swindle, extortion, sham, double-cross, hoax, cheat, ploy, ruse, hoodwink, confidence trick. Fraud on internet, constitutes about one-third of all cyber-crimes. It is the most profitable business on the Internet.

Some of the major areas of fraud and cheating on the Internet include:

a. Misuse of credit cards by obtaining passwords by hacking,
b. Bogus investment/get rich schemes,
c. Deceptive investment newsletters containing false information about companies,

d. Non delivery of goods purchased from online auctions and websites,
e. Misappropriation & transfer of funds etc.

Laws relating to cyber fraud & cheating

- IPC section 405, 406 (criminal breach of trust)- Imprisonment up to three years, or with fine, or both.
- IPC section 468 (Forgery)- Imprisonment up to seven years and fine.
- IPC section 477 A (Falsification of accounts)- Imprisonment up to seven years, or with fine, or both.
- IPC section 482 (using a false property)- Imprisonment up to one year, or with fine, or both.

Defamation

The term defamation is used to define the injury that is caused to the reputation of a person in the eyes of a third person. The injury can be done by words oral or written, or by signs or by visible representations. Cyber defamation is publishing of defamatory material against another person with the help of computers or internet. If someone publishes some defamatory statement about some other person on a website or send emails containing defamatory material to other persons with the intention to defame the other person would amount to cyber defamation. The harm caused to a person by publishing a defamatory statement about him on a website is widespread and irreparable as the information is available to the entire world.

Laws relating to defamation

1. **Section 499 of IPC:** Section 499 of IPC says that whoever, by words either spoken or intended to be read, or by

signs or by visible representations, makes or publishes any imputation concerning any person intending to harm. The offence of defamation is punishable and imprisonment up to 2 years or fine or both.

2. **Section 469 of IPC**: Section 469 of IPC says that whoever commits forgery, intending that the document or electronic record forged shall harm the reputation of any party, or knowing that it is likely to be used for that purpose shall be punished with imprisonment of either description for a term which may extend to three years and shall also be liable to fine.
3. **Section 66A**: The section 66A of the Information Act, 2000 does not specifically deal with the offence of cyber defamation but it makes punishable the act of sending grossly offensive material for causing insult, injury or criminal intimidation.

Defamation v. Freedom of speech

Freedom of speech and expression, as provided by the Constitution under Article 19 (1) (a), provides that all citizens shall have the right to freedom of speech and expression. However, such freedom is subject to reasonable restriction. The protection of reputation of another person falls within the ambit of reasonable restriction and any comment or remark which hampers the reputation of another person (unless the statement is true) would invite liability under the law of defamation.

Harassment

Online harassment may involve threatening or harassing emails, instant messages, or posting information online. It targets a specific person either by directly contacting them or by disseminating their personal information, causing them distress, fear, or anger. It can involve behaviors such as:

1. Sending unsolicited and/or threatening e-mail.
2. Encouraging others to send the victim unsolicited and/or threatening e-mail or to overwhelm the victim with e-mail messages.
3. Sending viruses by e-mail (electronic sabotage).
4. Spreading rumors.
5. Making defamatory comments about the victim online.
6. Sending negative messages directly to the victim.
7. Impersonating the victim online by sending an inflammatory, controversial or enticing message which causes others to respond negatively to the victim.
8. Harassing the victim during a live chat.
9. Leaving abusive messages online, including social media sites.
10. Sending the victim pornography or other graphic material that is knowingly offensive.
11. Creating online content that depicts the victim in negative ways.

E-mail Abuse

Email Abuse, also known as junk email, is a type of electronic spam where unsolicited messages are sent by email. Many email spam messages are commercial in nature but may also contain disguised links that appear to be for familiar websites but in fact lead to phishing web sites or sites that are hosting malware. Spam email may also include malware as scripts or other executable file attachments (like Trojans).

Other IT Act Offences-The offences included in the IT Act 2000 are as follows:

- Tampering with the computer source documents.
- Hacking computer system.
- Publishing of information which is obscene in electronic form.
- Penalty for misrepresentation
- Penalty for breach of confidentiality and privacy
- Penalty for publishing false digital signature certificate
- Publication for fraudulent purpose
- Act to apply for offence or contravention committed outside India
- Confiscation
- Penalties or confiscation not to interfere with other punishments.
- Power to investigate offences.

Monetary penalties

Monetary penalty is a civil penalty imposed by a regulator for a contravention of an Act, regulation or by-law. It is issued upon discovery of an unlawful event and is payable subject only to any rights of review. It is regulatory in nature, rather than criminal and is intended to secure compliance with a regulatory scheme, and it can be employed with the use of other administrative sanctions, such as demerit points and license suspensions.

S No	Section	Offence	Punishment
1	65	Tampering with Computer Source Code	Imprisonment up to 3 years or fine up to Rs 2 lakhs
2	66	Computer Related Offences	Imprisonment up to 3 years or fine up to Rs 5 lakhs
3	66-A	Sending offensive messages through Communication service, etc...	Imprisonment up to 3 years and fine
4	66-B	Dishonestly receiving stolen computer resource or communication device	Imprisonment up to 3 years and/or fine up to Rs. 1 lakh
5	66-C	Identity Theft	Imprisonment of either description up to 3 years and/or fine up to Rs. 1 lakh
6	66-D	Cheating personation by using computer resource	Imprisonment of either description up to 3 years and /or fine up to Rs. 1 lakh
7	66-E	Violation of Privacy	Imprisonment up to 3 years and /or fine up to Rs. 2 lakh
8	66-F	Cyber Terrorism	Imprisonment extend to imprisonment for Life
9	67	Publishing or transmitting obscene material in electronic form	On first Conviction, imprisonment up to 3 years and/or fine up to Rs. 5 lakhs On Subsequent Conviction imprisonment up to 5 years and/or fine up to Rs. 10 lakhs
10	71	Misrepresentation to the Controller to the Certifying Authority	Imprisonment up to 2 years and/ or fine up to Rs. 1 lakh.
11	72	Breach of Confidentiality and privacy	Imprisonment up to 2 years and/or fine up to Rs. 1 lakh.
12	72-A	Disclosure of information in breach of lawful contract	Imprisonment up to 3 years and/or fine up to Rs. 5 lakh.
13	73	Publishing electronic Signature Certificate false in certain particulars	Imprisonment up to 2 years and/or fine up to Rs. 1 lakh
14	74	Publication for fraudulent purpose	Imprisonment up to 2 years and/or fine up to Rs. 1 lakh

Table 3.1: Monetary penalties

Jurisdiction and Cyber Crimes

The whole trouble with internet jurisdiction is the presence of multiple parties in various parts of the world who have only a virtual nexus with each other. Then, if one party wants to sue the other, where can he sue?

Traditional requirement generally encompasses two areas: -

- The Place where the defendant resides.
- Where the cause of action arises.

However, in the context of the internet or cyberspace (cyber-space is the electronic medium of computer networks, in which online communication takes place), both these are difficult to establish with any certainty. Considering the lack of physical boundaries on the internet, is it possible to reach out beyond the court's geographic boundaries to haul a defendant into its court for conduct in "Cyberspace". Issues of this nature have contributed to the complete confusion and contradictions that plague judicial decisions in the area of internet jurisdiction. Accordingly, in each case, a determination should be made as to where an online presence will subject the user to jurisdiction in a distant state or a foreign company.

As such, a single transaction may involve the laws of at least three jurisdictions:

- The laws of the state/nation in which the user resides,
- The laws of the state/nation that apply where the server hosting the transaction is located.
- The laws of the state/nation which apply to the person or business with whom the transaction takes place.

Jurisdiction by Information Technology Act 2000

Cyber law is the part of the overall legal system that deals with the internet, cyberspace, and their respective legal issues. Cyber law covers a fairly broad area covering several subtopics including freedom of expression, access to and usage of the internet, and online privacy. Generally, cyber law is referred to as the law of the Internet. The Information Technology Act, 2000 or ITA, 2000 or IT Act, was notified on October 17, 2000.

Cyber-crime

Cyber-crime is a crime which is conducted by the use of computer, electronic devices, and network (Internet) to offences against individual or group of individuals. A person, who is involved in such type of crime, called as cyber-criminal.

Types of cyber-crime:

1. Hacking
2. Spoofing
3. Salami Attack
4. Spam
5. Malware dissemination
6. Denial of Service
7. Software Piracy
8. Threatening
9. Forgery
10. Obscene or Offensive
11. Cyber Terrorism Content
12. Drug Trafficking
13. Pornography
14. Cyber Stalking
15. Fraud
16. Cyber Defamation
17. Phishing

Nature of criminality

The focus on crime is more evident in the study of criminology. In the definition of criminology, it has been described as the "systematic study of the nature, extent and control of law-breaking behavior". The focus on the assessment of the concept of crime is dealt by the aspect of 'criminology'. The nature of crime is increasingly changing largely because of the changes in the society and the environment. Today, a crime cannot be viewed on a single perspective alone. The concept of crime is explained on the basis of different contending perspectives or theories. Two of the most popular perspective that explains the nature of crime is its condition as being a social construct and being an individual criminality.

A. **Crime as a social construct**

It has been believed that criminality could be avoided if there are only prerequisites. Among these prerequisites include presence of very good living conditions, real free will, not maltreatment from the direct and indirect environment, family with principles and a job which can be considered as dignified. In the absence of the noted prerequisites, it is likely that problematic or troubled individuals can be lured into becoming criminals. Because of this, there is a need for the society to all the members the favorable living conditions. If not, it would be almost unavoidable for the individuals to commit criminal acts.

A. **An individual criminality**

On the other hand, there is also the perspective that the individuals' criminality is not a question. Scholars and the researchers alike argue that genetic factories such as the wrong genes and chromosomes can drive the individuals to absence of self-control, aggressive attitudes as well as generally criminal behavior.

Strategies to tackle cyber-crime and trends

- **Protect your most visible asset-** Websites are the most visible and vulnerable part of a company's infrastructure. Attackers can scan the Internet nonstop in search of weaknesses; companies should not overlook this vulnerable entry point in their cyber security defense strategy. Products like malware and vulnerability scanners and web-application firewalls can help you guard this important asset that is the face of your brand.

- **Focus on effects**- It's clear that organizations can't prevent 100 percent of intrusions. A sophisticated and determined adversary will eventually get in. This is why companies should focus on detecting the effects (also called indicators of attack) of malware and adversary activity.

- **Remember that people are your weakest link**- Even the most advanced technology can't prevent a great employee from accidentally opening your doors to cybercrime. These unintentional slip-ups happen; combat them by reiterating common sense practices to all of your employees.

- Prevention is always better than cure. It is always better to take certain precautions while working on the net. One should make them a part of his cyber life.

- One should avoid disclosing any personal information to strangers, the person whom they don't know, via e-mail or while chatting or any social networking site.

- One must avoid sending any photograph to strangers by online as misusing or modification of photograph incidents increasing day by day.

- An updated anti-virus software to guard against virus attacks should be used by all the netizens and should also keep back up volumes so that one may not suffer data loss in case of virus contamination.

- A person should never send his credit card number or debit card number to any site that is not secured, to guard against frauds.

4

The Indian Evidence Act of 1872 v. Information Technology Act, 2000

The Indian Evidence Act of 1872

The Indian Evidence Act, originally passed in India by the Imperial Legislative Council in1 September, 1872, during the British Raj, contains a set of rules and allied issues governing admissibility of evidence in the Indian courts of law.

'Evidence' is derived from the Latin term "Evidere" which means - "to show clearly, to make plainly certain, to ascertain, to prove". The word 'evidence' includes all legal means, exclusive of mere arguments, which tend to prove or disprove any matter of fact, the truth of which is submitted to judicial investigation.

The enactment and adoption of the Indian Evidence Act was a path-breaking judicial measure introduced in India, which changed the entire system of concepts pertaining to admissibility of evidences in the Indian courts of law. Until then, the rules of evidences were based on the traditional legal systems of different social groups and communities of India and were different for different people depending on caste, community, faith and social position. The Indian Evidence Act introduced a standard set of law applicable to all Indians.

This Act is divided into three parts and there are 11 chapters in this Act.

Part 1

Part 1 deals with relevancy of the facts. There are two chapters under this part: the first chapter is a preliminary chapter which introduces to the Evidence Act and the second chapter specifically deals with the relevancy of the facts.

Part 2

Part 2 consists of chapters from 3 to 6. Chapter 3 deals with facts which need not be proved, chapter 4 deals with oral evidence, chapter 5 deals with documentary evidence and chapter 6 deals with circumstances when documentary evidence has been given preference over the oral evidence.

Part 3

The last part, that is part 3, consists of chapter 7 to chapter 11. Chapter 7 talks about the burden of proof. Chapter 8 talks about estoppels, chapter 9 talks about witnesses, chapter 10 talks about examination of witnesses, and last chapter which is chapter 11 talks about improper admission and rejection of evidence.

IT Act 2000

Cyber law is the part of the overall legal system that deals with the internet, cyberspace, and their respective legal issues. Cyber law covers a fairly broad area covering several subtopics including freedom of expression, access to and usage of the internet, and online privacy.

In 1996, the United Nations Commission on International Trade Law (UNCITRAL) adopted the model law on electronic commerce (e-commerce) to bring uniformity in the law in different countries. Further, the General Assembly of the United Nations recommended that all countries must consider this model law before making changes to their own laws. India became the 12th country to enable cyber law after it passed the Information Technology Act, 2000.The Information Technology Act, 2000 or ITA, 2000 or IT Act, was notified on October 17, 2000. It is the law that deals with cyber-crime and electronic commerce in India.

The Information Technology (IT) Act 2000 was amended to allow for the admissibility of digital evidence. An amendment to the Indian Evidence Act 1872, the Indian Penal Code 1860 and the Banker's Book Evidence Act 1891 provides the legislative framework for transactions in electronic world.

Evidence is not only limited to that found on computers but may also extend to include evidence on digital devices such as telecommunication or electronic multimedia devices. The e-EVIDENCE can be found in e-mails, digital photographs, ATM transaction logs, word processing, documents, instant message histories, files saved from accounting programs, spreadsheets, internet browser histories databases, Contents of computer memory, Computer backups, Computer printouts, Global Positioning System tracks, Logs from a hotel's electronic door locks, Digital video or audio files.

Status of electronic records as evidence

Digital evidence or electronic evidence is any probative information stored or transmitted in digital form. Before accepting digital evidence, it is vital that the determination of its relevance, veracity and authenticity be ascertained by the court and to establish if the fact is hearsay or a copy is preferred to the original. Digital Evidence is “information of probative value that is stored or transmitted in binary form”.

Evidence is not only limited to that found on computers but may also extend to include evidence on digital devices such as telecommunication or electronic multimedia devices. The e-EVIDENCE can be found in e-mails, digital photographs, ATM transaction logs, word processing, documents, instant message histories, files saved from accounting programs, spreadsheets, internet browser histories databases, contents of computer memory, computer backups, computer printouts, global positioning system tracks, logs from a hotel’s electronic door locks, digital video or audio files etc.

The term ‘electronic records’ has been given the same meaning as that assigned to it under the IT Act. IT Act provides for "data, record or data generated, image or sound stored, received or sent in an electronic form or microfilm or computer-generated microfiche".

Computer forensics is a branch of forensic science pertaining to legal evidence found in computers and digital storage mediums. Computer forensics is also known as digital forensics. The goal of computer forensics is to explain the current state of a digital artifact.

Proof and management of electronic records

ISO standard 15489: 2001 defines Records Management (RM) as the field of management responsible for the efficient and systematic control of the creation, receipt, maintenance, use and disposition of records, including the processes for capturing and maintaining evidence and information about business activities and transactions in the form of records. Electronic Records Management (ERM) ensures your organization has the records it needs when they are needed.

Essential records management capabilities include assigning unique identifiers to individual records, providing safeguards against unauthorized changes being made to those records, and creating an unbreakable audit trail for reasons of accountability and e-Discovery.

To prove electronic record/evidence, victim can provide the original electronic media as primary evidence in court or its copy by secondary evidence U/s 65A/65B of Evidence Act. Thus, in the case of CD, DVD, memory card etc. containing secondary evidence, the same shall be accompanied by the certificate in terms of section 65B obtained at the time of taking the document, without which, the secondary evidence pertaining to that electronic record, is inadmissible.

Relevancy, Admissibility and Probative Value of E-Evidence

Relevancy

The word relevant means, any two realities to which it is connected and identified with one another. Relevancy refers to the degree of connection and probative value between a fact that is given in evidence and the issue to be proved. Relevancy of facts had been provided from Section 5 to 55 of Evidence Act 1950.

In laws of evidence, relevant facts could depict any set of closely interrelated facts, to the extent that they rely on each other to establish an event. These facts make the event more or less likely than it would be in their absence. Relevancy is based on logic, admissibility only relies on lawful pertinence, i.e., whether a fact can be permitted in court on the basis of the Evidence Act.

A fact could appear sensibly pertinent, however may not be admissible in court. For example, police confessions, hearsay statements, privileged communications, etc are relevant, but not admissible. They are barred by positive rules of law, determined by the statute and the court's interpretation of the same. Naturally, relevancy must be established before admissibility can be dealt with. For the sake of brevity, courts only let in the facts which have a high degree of probative value, affording clarity to the case.

Two leading principles on relevance

1. That nothing is to be received which is not logically probative of some matter requiring to be proved.
2. That everything which is thus probative should come in, unless a clear ground of policy or law excludes it. Relevancy exists as a relation between an item of evidence and a proposition sought to be proved."

Admissibility and Probative value of E-Evidence

Admissibility means that the facts which are relevant are only admissible by the Court. According to section 136 of the Indian Evidence Act, 1872, however, the final discretion on the admissibility of evidence lies with the judge.

Admissibility involves the process whereby the court determines whether the Law of Evidence permits that relevant evidence to be received by the court. The concept of admissibility is often distinguished from relevancy. Relevancy is determined by logic and common sense, practical or human experience, and knowledge of affairs. On the other hand, the admissibility of evidence, depends first on the concept of relevancy of a sufficiently high degree of probative value, and secondly, on the fact that the evidence tendered does not infringe any of the exclusionary rules that may be applicable to it. Relevancy is not primarily dependent on rules of law but admissibility is founded on law.

Section 136 states that: "When either party proposes to give evidence of any fact, the Judge may ask the party proposing to give the evidence in what manner the alleged fact, if proved, would be relevant; and the Judge shall admit the evidence if he thinks that the fact, if proved, would be relevant, and not otherwise. If the fact proposed to be proved is one of which evidence is admissible only upon proof of some other fact, such last- mentioned fact must be proved before evidence is given of the fact first- mentioned, unless the party undertakes to give proof of such fact, and the court is satisfied with such undertaking".

S No.	Relevancy	Admissibility
1	When facts are so related as to render the existence or non-existence of other facts probable according to common course of events or human conduct, they are called relevant.	When facts have been declared to be legally relevant under I.E. Act, they become admissible.
2	It is founded on logic and human experience.	It is founded on law not on logic.
3	The question regarding relevancy has been enunciated in Sec.5 to Sec.55 of I.E. Act.	The question of admissibility is provided in Sec.56 and 136.
4	It signifies as to what facts are necessary to prove or disprove a fact in issue.	It is a decisive factor between relevancy and proof.
5	It merely implies the relevant facts.	It is the effect.
6	The court may apply its discretion.	There is no scope for the court to apply discretion.
7	All admissible facts are relevant.	All relevant facts are not admissible. Only legally relevant facts are admissible.

Table 4.1: Difference between Relevancy and Admissibility

Proving digital signature

A digital signature is an electronic signature that can be used to authenticate the identity of the sender of a message or the signer of a document, and to ensure that the original content of the message or document that has been sent is unchanged. Digital signatures are easily transportable, cannot be imitated by someone else, and can be automatically time-stamped. A digital signature can be used with any kind of message, whether it is encrypted or plaintext. Thus Digital Signatures provide the following three features-

A. **Authentication-** Digital signatures are used to authenticate the source of messages. The ownership of a digital signature key is bound to a specific user and thus a valid signature shows that the message was sent by that user.
B. **Integrity-** In many scenarios, the sender and receiver of a message need assurance that the message has not been altered during transmission. Digital Signatures provide this feature by using cryptographic message digest functions.
C. **Non Repudiation–** Digital signatures ensure that the sender who has signed the information cannot at a later time deny having signed it.

How digital signatures work

The digital signatures require a key pair (asymmetric key pairs, mathematically related large numbers) called the public and private keys. Just as physical keys are used for locking and unlocking, in cryptography, the equivalent functions are encryption and decryption. The private key is kept confidential with the owner usually on a secure media like crypto smart card or crypto token. The public key is shared with everyone. Information encrypted by a private key can only be decrypted using the corresponding public key.

In order to digitally sign an electronic document, the sender uses his/her private key. In order to verify the digital signature, the recipient uses the sender's Public Key.

Let us understand how the digital signatures work based on an example. Assume you are going to send the draft of a contract to your lawyer in another town. You want to give your lawyer the assurance that it was unchanged from what you had sent and that it is really from you.

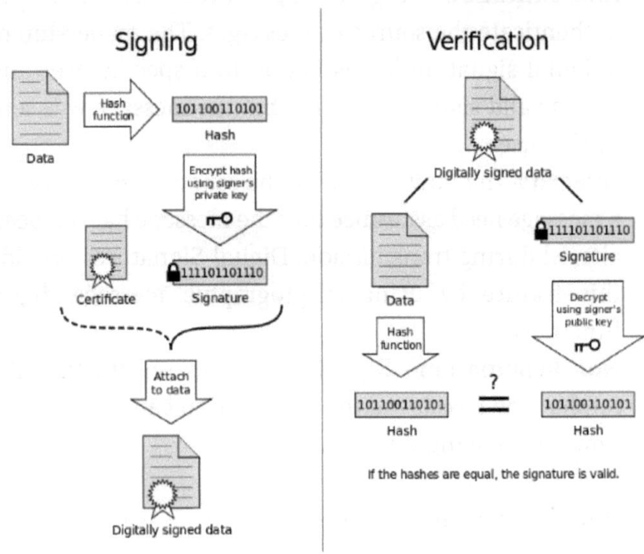

Figure 4.1: Working of digital signature

The Indian Information Technology Act 2000 came into effect from October 17, 2000. One of the primary objectives of the Information Technology Act of 2000 was to promote the use of digital signatures for authentication in e-commerce & e-Governance. Towards facilitating this, the office of Controller of Certifying Authorities (CCA) was set up in 2000. The CCA licenses Certifying Authorities (CAs) to issue Digital Signature Certificates (DSC) under the IT Act 2000. The standards and practices to be followed were defined in the Rules and Regulations under the Act and the Guidelines that are issued by CCA from time to time. The Root Certifying Authority of India (RCAI) was set up by the CCA to serve as the root of trust in the hierarchical Public Key Infrastructure (PKI) model that has been set up in the country.

Proof of electronic agreements

An e-contract is an agreement created and signed in electronic form (no paper is used). An e-Contract, or electronic contract, is a legal document created and signed online. It is essentially a digital version of a traditional paper contract. As with paper contracts, e-Contracts agreements are signed by two parties. They are enforceable and legally binding documents that are typically used regarding employment, sales, services, or tenancy. With a typical paper contract, one party drafts an “offer” and the other party reads over it. If both parties agree to the terms and conditions listed in this initial offer, they will each sign the document and it becomes a valid contract. Each party must hold up to their end of the agreement or they face the risk of legal recourse.

An example is a contract that you write on your computer and email to a business associate and that the business associate emails back with an electronic signature indicating acceptance. An e-contract can also be in the form of a "click to agree" contract, which commonly comes with downloaded software: The user clicks an "I agree" button on a page containing the terms of the software license before being able to complete the transaction.

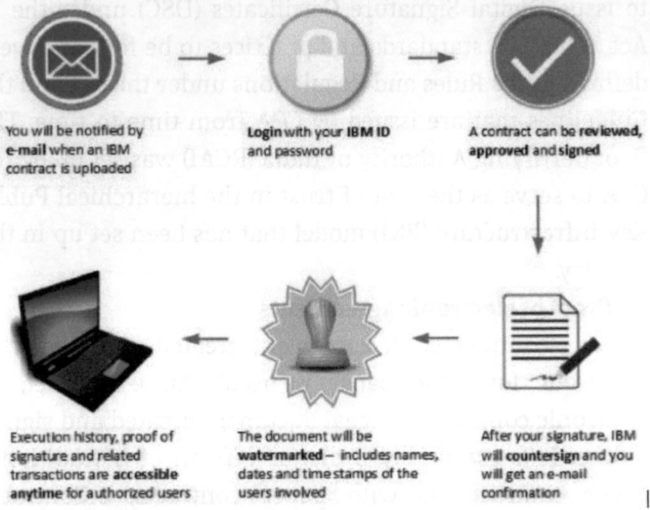

Figure 4.2: Example of Online Agreement

Admissibility (Proof) of E-agreements as evidence

Under the Evidence Act, 1872, an e-agreement has the same legal effect as a paper based agreement. The definition of "evidence" as provided under section 3 of the Evidence Act includes "all documents including electronic records produced for the inspection of the court".

Section 65B(1) of the Evidence Act provides that any information contained in an electronic record which is printed on a paper, stored, recorded or copied in optical or magnetic media produced by a computer shall be deemed to be also a document and shall be admissible in any proceedings, without further proof or production of the original, as evidence of any contents of the original or of any fact stated therein of which direct evidence would be admissible.

Section 84A12 provides for the presumption that a contract has been concluded where the parties' digital signatures are affixed to an electronic record that purports to be an agreement.

Section 85B of the Evidence Act provides that where a security procedure has been applied to an electronic record at a specific time, the record is deemed tobe a secure electronic record from such time until the time of verification. Unless the contrary is proved, the court is to presume that a secure electronic record has not been altered since obtaining secure status. The provisions relating to a secure digital signature are set out in section 15 of the IT Act.

Proving Electronic Messages

As more and more information is moved around the organization and the world using the growing E-mail and electronic messaging infrastructure, what technologies are available to ensure that these messages are protected, that the recipient is positive of the sender's identity and that messages are not damaged or altered in transit.

On September 5, 2007, the Unsolicited Electronic Messages Act 2007 came into force. The Act prohibits the sending of unsolicited commercial electronic messages. Email, instant messaging, SMS, multimedia messaging services are covered by the Act. It does not cover voice calls (real, recorded or synthetic) or facsimiles.

Under section 88A, it is presumed that an electronic message forwarded by a sender through an electronic mail server to an addressee corresponds with the message fed into the sender's computer for transmission. However, there is no presumption regarding the person who sent the message.

5

Tools and Methods in Cybercrime

Proxy servers

A proxy server is a server (a computer system or an application) that acts as an intermediary for requests from clients seeking resources from other servers. A client connects to the proxy server, requesting some service, such as a file, connection, web page, or other resource available from a different server and the proxy server evaluates the request as a way to simplify and control its complexity. Today, most proxies are web proxies, facilitating access to content on the World Wide Web, providing anonymity and may be used to bypass IP address blocking.

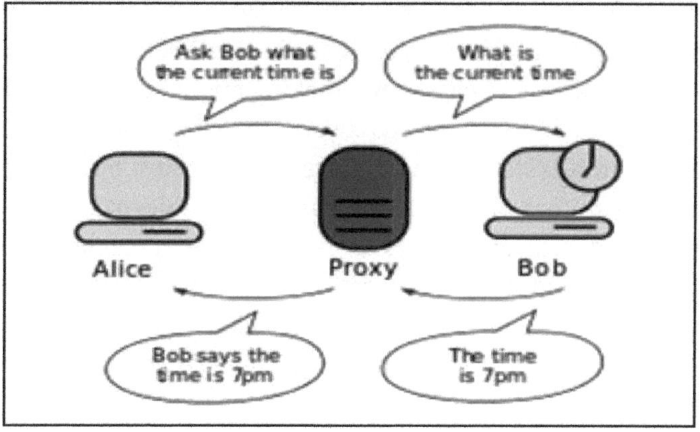

Figure 5.1: Communication between computer and proxy server

Anonymizers

An Anonymizers or an anonymous proxy is a tool that attempts to make activity on the Internet untraceable. It is a proxy server (computer) that acts as an intermediary and privacy shield between a client computer and the rest of the Internet. It accesses the Internet on the user's behalf, protecting personal information by hiding the client computer's identifying information. There are many reasons for using Anonymizers. Anonymizers minimize the risk. They can be used to prevent identity theft, or to protect search histories from public disclosure. Anonymizers can help in allowing free access to all of the internet content, but cannot help against persecution for accessing the Anonymizers website itself.

Password cracking

Password cracking is the process of recovering passwords from data that have been stored in or transmitted by a computer system. A common approach (brute force attack) is to guess the password and check them against an available cryptographic hash of the password.

The purpose of password cracking might be help a user to recover a forgotten password to gain unauthorized access to a system, or as a preventive measure by system administrators to check for easily traceable passwords. Password cracking refers to various measures used to discover computer passwords. This is usually accomplished by recovering passwords from data stored in, or transported from, a computer system. Password cracking is done by either repeatedly guessing the password, usually through a computer algorithm in which the computer tries numerous combinations until the password is successfully discovered.

Key loggers

A key logger is a piece of software or a hardware device that logs every key press on keyboard. It can capture personal messages, passwords, credit card numbers etc. Key loggers are generally installed by malware, but they may also be installed by protective parents, jealous spouses, or employers who want to monitor their employees. Hardware key loggers are perfect for corporate espionage.

Key loggers can pose a serious threat to users, as they can be used to intercept passwords and other confidential information entered via the keyboard. As a result, cybercriminals can get PIN codes and account numbers for financial accounts, passwords of email and social networking accounts and then uses this information to take user's money, steal user's identity and possibly extort information and money from user's friends and family.

Types of Key l

A. **Software Key loggers: Software key loggers are computer programs that install onto user device's hard drive.**
B. **Hardware Key loggers: Hardware key loggers are physical components built-in or connected to user device. Some hardware methods may be able to track keystrokes without even being connected to user device.**

Best practices for detecting and removing key loggers

1. **Monitor resource allocation, processes and data**
2. **Keep antivirus and anti-Root kit protection up to date**
3. **Use anti-key logger software**
4. **Consider virtual onscreen keyboards**
5. **Disable self-running files on external devices**
6. **Have a strong password policy**

Spyware

Spyware is the term given to a category of software which aims to steal personal or organizational information. It is done by performing a set of operations without appropriate user permissions. General actions of a spyware include advertising, collection of personal information and changing user configuration settings of the computer. A Spyware is generally classified into adware, tracking cookies, system monitors and Trojans.

The most common way for a spyware to get into the computer through freeware and shareware as a bundled hidden component. Once a spyware gets successfully installed, it starts sending the data from that computer in the background to some other place. Spywares are usually used to give popup advertisements based on user's habits and search history. One of the simplest and most popular, yet dangerous is Key loggers. It is used to record the keystrokes which could be fatal as it can record passwords, credit card information etc. In some shared networks and corporate computers, it is also intentionally installed to track user activities.

Presence of spyware in a computer can create a lot of other troubles as spyware intended to monitor the computer, spywares can change user preferences, permissions and also administrative rights, resulting in users being locked out of their own computer and in some cases, can also result in full data losses. Spyware running in the background can also amount to increased number of processes and result in frequent crashes. It also often slows down a computer.

Virus

A computer virus is malicious code that replicates by copying itself to another program. Virus can replicate in computer boot sector, document, hard disk or they can infect the files. The virus requires someone to knowingly or unknowingly spread the infection without the knowledge or permission of a user or system administrator.

A virus can be spread by opening an email attachment, clicking on an executable file, visiting an infected website or viewing an infected website advertisement. It can also be spread through infected removable storage devices, such USB drives. Once a virus has infected the host, it can infect other system software or resources modify or disable core functions or applications, as well as copy, delete or encrypt data. Some virus begins replicating as soon as they infect the host, while other virus will lie dormant until a specific trigger causes malicious code to be executed by the device or system.

Types of virus

- **File infectors**- Some file infector virus attach themselves to program files, usually selected.com or .exe files. Some can infect any program for which execution is requested, including .sys, .ovl, .prg, and .mnufiles. When the program is loaded, the virus is loaded as well.
- **Macro virus**- These viruses specifically target macro language commands in applications like Microsoft Word and other programs. In Microsoft Word, macros are saved sequences for commands or keystrokes that are embedded in the documents. Macro virus can add their malicious code to the legitimate macro sequences in a Word file.

Microsoft disabled macros by default in more recent versions of Word; as a result, hackers have used social engineering schemes to convince targeted users to enable macros and launch the virus. As macro virus have seen a resurgence in recent years, Microsoft added a new feature in Office 2016 that allows security managers to selectively enable macro use for trusted workflows only, as well as block macros across an organization.

- **Overwrite virus**- Some virus are designed specifically to destroy a file or application's data. After infecting a system, an overwrite virus begins overwriting files with its own code. This virus can target specific files or applications or systematically overwrite all files on an infected device. An overwrite virus can install new code in files and applications that programs them to spread the virus to additional files, applications and systems.

- **Polymorphic virus**- A polymorphic virus is a type of malware that has the ability to change or mutate its underlying code without changing its basic functions or features. This process helps a virus evade detection from many antimalware and threat detection products that rely on identifying signatures of malware; once a polymorphic virus signature is identified by a security product; the virus can then alter itself so that it will no longer be detected using that signature.
- **Resident virus**- This type of virus embeds itself in the memory of a system. The original virus program isn't needed to infect new files or applications; even if the original virus is deleted, the version stored in memory can be activated when the operating system loads a specific application or function. Resident virus is problematic because they can evade antivirus and antimalware software by hiding in the system's RAM.
- **Rootkit virus**- A Rootkit virus is a type of malware that installs an unauthorized Rootkit on an infected system, giving attackers full control of the system with the ability to fundamentally modify or disable functions and programs. Rootkit viruses were designed to bypass antivirus software, which typically scanned only applications and files. More recent versions of major antivirus and antimalware programs include Rootkit scanning to identify and mitigate these types of viruse.
- **System or boot record infectors**- This virus infect executable code found in certain system areas on a disk.

They attach to the DOS boot sector on diskettes and USB thumb drives or the Master Boot Record on hard disks. In a typical attack scenario, the victim receives storage device that contains a boot disk virus. When the victim's operating system is running, files on the external storage device can infect the system; rebooting the system will trigger the boot disk virus.

An infected storage device connected to a computer can modify or even replace the existing boot code on the infected system so that when the system is booted next, the virus will be loaded and run immediately as part of the master boot record.

Worms

A computer worm is a standalone malware computer program that replicates itself in order to spread to other computers. Often, it uses a computer network to spread itself, relying on security failures on the target computer to access it. Worms almost always cause at least some harm to the network, even if only by consuming bandwidth, whereas virus almost always corrupt or modify files on a targeted computer.

Worms can modify and delete files, and they can even inject additional malicious software onto a computer. Sometimes a computer worm's purpose is only to make copies of itself over and over depleting system resources, such as hard drive space or bandwidth, by overloading a shared network. In addition to wreaking havoc on a computer's resources, worms can also steal data, install a backdoor, and allow a hacker to gain control over a computer and its system settings.

How to detect a computer worm

It can be hard to detect the presence of a worm. Signs that indicate a worm might be present include the following symptoms:

- Computer performance issues over time, limited computing bandwidth with no apparent explanation
- System freezing or crashing unexpectedly
- Unusual system behavior, including programs that execute or terminate without user interaction
- Unusual sounds, images or messages
- The sudden appearance of unfamiliar files or icons, or the unexpected disappearance of files or icons
- Warning messages from the operating system or antivirus software
- Email messages sent to contacts that the user didn't actually send.

Difference between Worms and Virus

S. No.	Worms	Virus
1.	A Worm is a form of malware that replicates itself and can spread to different computers via Network.	A Virus is a malicious executable code attached to another executable file which can be harmless or can modify or delete data.
2.	The main objective of worms to eat the system resources.	The main objective of virus is to modify the information.
3.	It doesn't need a host to replicate from one computer to another.	It requires host is needed for spreading.
4.	It is less harmful as compared.	It is more harmful.
5.	Worms can be detected and removed by the Antivirus and firewall.	Antivirus software is used for protection against virus.
6.	Worms can be controlled by remote.	Virus can't be controlled by remote.
7.	Worms are executed via weaknesses in system.	Viruses are executed via executable files.
8.	Morris Worm, Storm Worm and SQL Slammer are some of the examples of worms.	Resident and Non-resident viruses are two types of virus.
9.	It does not needs human action to replicate.	It needs human action to replicate.
10.	Its spreading speed is faster.	Its spreading speed is slower as compared.

Table 5.1: Difference between Worms and Virus

Trojan horse

A Trojan horse or Trojan is a type of malware that is often disguised as legitimate software. Trojans can be employed by cyber-thieves and hackers trying to gain access to users' systems. Users are typically tricked by some form of social engineering into loading and executing Trojans on their systems. Once activated, Trojans can enable cyber-criminals to spy on victim, steal sensitive data, and gain backdoor access to system. These actions can include:

- Deleting data
- Blocking data
- Modifying data
- Copying data
- Disrupting the performance of computers or computer networks. Unlike computer viruses and worms, Trojans are not able to self-replicate.

Protection against Trojan horse

1. **Be cautious about downloads:** Never download or install software from unknown source.
2. **Be aware of phishing threats:** Never open an attachment, click a link, or run a program sent on email from unknown person.
3. **Update operating system's software as soon as the updates are available:** In addition to operating system

updates, user should also check for updates on other software uses on his computer. Updates often include security patches to keep safe from emerging threats.

4. **Don't visit unsafe websites:** Look out for sites that have security certificates– their URL should start with https:// rather than http:// - the "s" stands for "secure" and there should be a padlock icon in the address bar too.
5. **Avoid clicking pop-ups and banners**: Don't click on unfamiliar, untrusted pop-ups and warnings. By clicking them, user's device can infect and then offering a magical programs to fix it. This is a common Trojan horse tactic.
6. **Protect accounts with complex, unique passwords**: A strong password is not easy to guess and ideally made up of a combination of upper- and lower-case letters, special characters, and numbers. Avoid using the same password across the board and change password regularly. A password manager tool is an excellent way to manage passwords.
7. **Keep personal information safe with firewalls:** Firewalls screen data that enters victim's device from the internet. While most operating systems come with a built-in firewall, it's also **a good idea to use a hardware firewall for complete protection.**

Backdoors

A backdoor is a malware type that negates normal authentication procedures to access a system. As a result, remote access is granted to resources within an application, such as databases and file servers, giving perpetrators the ability to remotely issue system commands and update malware. Backdoor installation is achieved by taking advantage of vulnerable components in a web application.

Once installed, detection is difficult as files tend to be highly obfuscated. Web server backdoors are used for a number of malicious activities, including:

- Data theft
- Website defacing
- Server hijacking
- The launching of distributed denial of service (DDoS) attacks
- Infecting website visitors (watering hole attacks)

DoS attack

A denial-of-service (DoS) is any type of attack where the attackers (hackers) attempt to prevent legitimate users from accessing the service. In a DoS attack, the attacker usually sends excessive messages asking the network or server to authenticate requests that have invalid return addresses. The network or server will not be able to find the return address of the attacker when sending the authentication approval, causing the server to wait before closing the connection. When the server closes the connection, the attacker sends more authentication messages with invalid return addresses. Hence, the process of authentication and server wait will begin again, keeping the network or server busy.

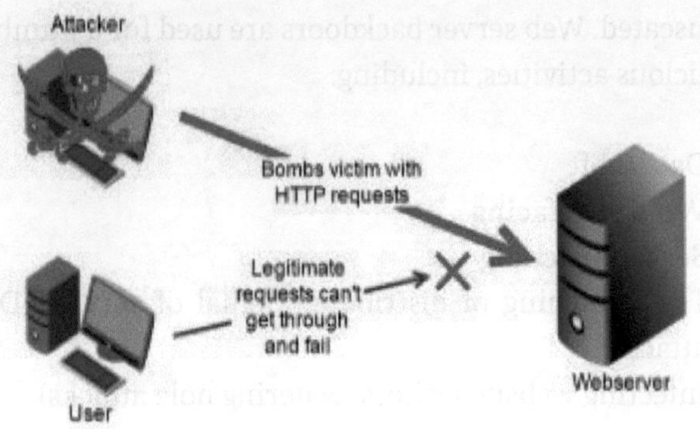

Figure 5.2: DoS attack

DDoS attack

A Distributed Denial of Service (DDoS) attack is an attempt to make an online service unavailable by overwhelming it with traffic from multiple sources. They target a wide variety of important resources, from banks to news websites, and present a major challenge to making sure people can publish and access important information.

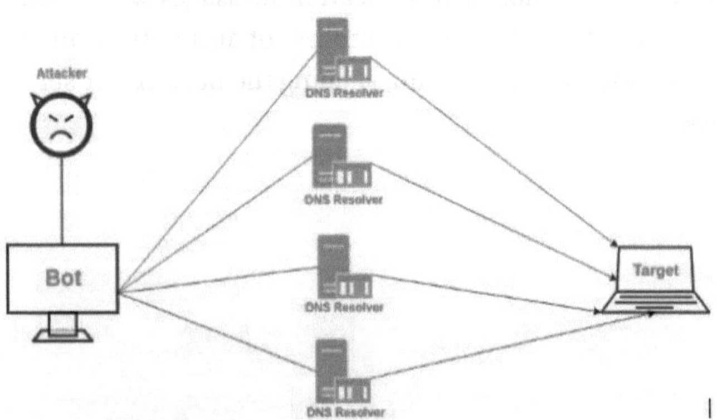

Figure 5.3: DDoS attack

Buffer overflow

Buffers are memory storage regions that temporarily hold data while it is being transferred from one location to another. A buffer overflow (or buffer overrun) occurs when the volume of data exceeds the storage capacity of the memory buffer. As a result, the program attempting to write the data to the buffer overwrites adjacent memory locations.

A buffer overflow, or buffer overrun, is a common software coding mistake that an attacker could exploit to gain access to system. A method of overloading is a predefined amount of space in a buffer, which can potentially overwrite and corrupts memory in data. To effectively mitigate buffer overflow vulnerabilities, it is important to understand what buffer overflows are, what dangers they pose to user applications, and what techniques attackers use to successfully exploit these vulnerabilities.

Attackers exploit buffer overflow issues by overwriting the memory of an application. This changes the execution path of the program, triggering a response that damages files or exposes private information. For example, an attacker may introduce extra code, sending new instructions to the application to gain access to IT systems.

Types of buffer overflow attacks

A. **Stack-based buffer overflows** are more common, and leverage stack memory that only exists during the execution time of a function.

B. **Heap-based attacks** are harder to carry out and involve flooding the memory space allocated for a program beyond memory used for current runtime operations.

Key concepts of buffer overflow

- This error occurs when there is more data in a buffer than it can handle, causing data to overflow into adjacent storage.
- This vulnerability can cause a system crash or, worse, create an entry point for a cyber-attack.
- C and C++ are more susceptible to buffer overflow.
- Secure development practices should include regular testing to detect and fix buffer overflows.
- These practices include automatic protection at the language level and bounds-checking at run- time.

Attack on wireless networks

Wireless attacks have become a very common security issue when it comes to networks. This is because such attacks can really get a lot of information that is being sent across a network and use it to commit some crimes in other networks. Every wireless network is very vulnerable to such kinds of attacks and it is therefore very important that all the necessary security measures are taken so as to prevent the mess that can be caused by such attacks.

These attacks are normally carried out to target information that is being shared through the networks. It is therefore very important to know of such attacks so that one is in a position to identify it in case it happens. Some of the common network attacks have been outlined below.

- **Rogue access points**-A rouge access point is basically an access point that has been added to one's network without one's knowledge. Victim totally has no idea about it. This is an access point that can create some very huge security concerns.
- **Jamming/Interference**- Wireless interference basically means disruption of victim's network. This is a very big challenge especially owing to the fact that wireless signals will always get disrupted. Such interference can be created by a Bluetooth headset, a microwave oven and a cordless phone. This makes transmission and receiving of wireless signals very difficult.
- **Evil twin**- A wireless evil twin mainly comes into play when criminals are trying to create rogue access points so as to gain access to the network or access to information that is being put through a network. Coming up with an evil twin is very simple since all one need to do is purchase a wireless access point, plug it into the network and configure it as exactly as the existing network. This is possible in open access points that do not have any passwords associated with them.
- **War driving**- War driving is a way that bad guys use so as to find access points wherever they can be. With the availability of free Wi-Fi connection and other GPS functionalities, they can drive around and obtain a very huge amount of information over a very short period of time. One can also use some special type of software to view all the different access points around victim.
- **Blue Jacking**- Blue jacking is a kind of illegal activity that is similar to hacking where attacker can be able to send unsolicited messages to another device via Bluetooth. This is considered spam for Bluetooth and one might end up seeing some pop-up messages on

victim's screen. Blue jacking is possible where a Bluetooth network is present and it is limit end to a distance of ten meters which is the distance a Bluetooth device can send a file to another device.

- **Bluesnarfing**- Bluesnarfing is far much more malicious than blue jacking since it involves using one's Bluetooth to steal information. This is where a Bluetooth enabled device is able to use the vulnerability on the Bluetooth network to be able to get into a mobile device to steal information such as contacts and images. This is a vulnerability that exposes the weakness and vulnerability with the Bluetooth network. This is an act that creates some very serious security issues since an individual can steal a file from one if he or she knows it.
- **War chalking**- War chalking is another method that was used to determine where user could get a wireless access signal. In this case, if an individual detected a wireless access point, he or she would make a drawing on the wall indicating that a wireless access point has been found. However, this is not currently used.
- **IV attack**- An IV attack is also known as an Initialization Vector attack. This is a kind of wireless network attack that can be quite a threat to one's network. This is because it causes some modification on the Initialization Vector of a wireless packet that is encrypted during transmission. After such an attack, the attacker can obtain much information about the plaintext of a single packet and generate another encryption key which he or she can use to decrypt other packets using the same Initialization Vector. With that kind of decryption key, attackers can use it to come up with a decryption table which they and use to decrypt every packet being sent across the network.

- **Near field communication**- Near field communication is a kind of wireless communication between devices like smart phones where people are able to send information to near filed communication compatible devices without the need to bring the devices in contact. This allows one device to collect information from another device that is in close range.

Phishing methods

Phishing is a type of social engineering attack often used to steal user data, including login credentials and credit card numbers. It occurs when an attacker, masquerading as a trusted entity, dupes a victim into opening an email, instant message, or text message. Some key points about phishing-

- **Planning**- Phishers decide which business to target and determine how to get e-mail addresses for the customers of that business. They often use the same mass-mailing and address collection techniques as spammers.
- **Setup**- Once they know which business to spoof and who their victims are, Phishers creates methods for delivering the message and collecting the data. Most often, this involves e-mail addresses and a Web page.
- **Attack**- This is the step people are most familiar with the phisher sends a phony message that appears to be from a reputable source.
- **Collection**- Phishers record the information victims enter into Web pages or popup windows.
- **Identity theft and fraud**- The phishers use the information they've gathered to make illegal purchases or otherwise commit fraud. As many as a fourth of the victims never fully recover.

Phishing techniques: Popular phishing techniques used by hackers are:

1. Deceptive phishing

Deceptive phishing is the most common type of social media phishing. In a typical scenario, a phisher creates an account pretending to be the account of the victim. Next, the phisher sends friend requests to the friends of the victim as well as a message such as "I have abandoned my previous Facebook account. From now, please communicate with me through this account only". Afterwards, the phisher starts sending messages to the friends of the victim that demand the recipient to click on a link.

Examples of such messages include: A statement that the receiver of the message has a virus which can be deleted by signing up for a special anti-virus inspection conducted by the social network. A fictitious invoice can be cancelled by clicking on a link requesting the user to provide her/his personal information.

2. Content injection based phishing

The content-injection social network phishing refers to inserting malicious content in social networks. The malicious content can often be in the form of bogus posts (e.g., tweets, posts in the Facebook feed or in LinkedIn feed) published by users whose accounts were affected with rogue apps.

In many cases, the victims are unable to see the bogus posts posted by the malware apps on their behalf. The bogus posts, for example, may contain a photo of the account owner and the text: "I am in the hospital. If someone would like to help me, please sign up by clicking on the following link". When the victim clicks on the link, he/she will be requested to provide his/her personal data, which may be used by the phisher for committing identity theft and other scams.

3. Malware based phishing

Malware based phishing refers to a spread of phishing messages by using malware. For example, the Facebook account of a victim who installed a rogue Facebook app will automatically send messages to all the friends of the victim. Such messages often contain links allowing the receivers of the messages to install the rogue Facebook app on their computers or mobile devices. The best way to avoid the installation of rogue Facebook apps is to be very selective when installing any third-party Facebook applications.

For example, Facebook apps developed by unknown developers that request access to extensive information should be researched thoroughly. One method often used by phishers to "seduce" the Facebook users to install malware to their computer is to promise them that the malware will enable them to see a list of people who visited their Facebook profile page.

4. Men-in-the-middle phishing

A man-in-the-middle social network attack, also known as social network session hijacking attack, is a form of phishing in which the phisher positions himself between the user and a legitimate social network website. Messages intended for the legitimate social network website pass through the phisher who can inspect the messages and acquire valuable information.

used by the phisher for committing identity theft and other scams.

3. Malware based phishing

Malware based phishing refers to a spread of phishing messages by using malware. For example, the Facebook account of a victim who installed a rogue Facebook app will automatically send messages to all the friends of the victim. Such messages often contain links allowing the receivers of the messages to install the rogue Facebook app on their computers or mobile devices. The best way to avoid the installation of rogue Facebook apps is to be very selective while installing and downloading Facebook applications.

For example, Facebook apps developed by unknown developers that request access to extensive information should be researched thoroughly. One method often used by phishers to "seduce" the Facebook users to install malware to their computers is to promise them that the [illegible]

[illegible]

[illegible] attacks [illegible]

[illegible] for the login to the social network website pass [illegible] messages [illegible]

Author-1

Dr. Shiv Shakti Shrivastava
Professor (CSE)
Rabindranath Tagore University, Bhopal

Dr. Shiv Shakti Shrivastava is the Professor in Computer Science department in Rabindranath Tagore University, Bhopal. He has more than 20 years of experience. Under his guidance nine scholars has been awarded Ph.D., Six are also taking guidance and M.Tech.-MCA students also guided by him. He has published more than fourth five International & National papers in difference reputed journals. He has three patents and also trying funded patents. He is connected with many universities like Barkatullah Univ., RGPV, Makhanlal Univ., Bhoj Univ., and many more universities. He has taken many expert lectures, guest lecture, judge in different universities and colleges for technical and other events. He has been attended as guest in different webinars. He has completed three Faculty Development Program and also Successfully Completed training of the IEEE Xplore Digital Library. Ph.D. Thesis reviewed in many other universities. He has taken responsibilities as observers in technical events, examination and cultural activities in others universities.

Author-2

Prof. Ankit Chakrawarti

Assistant Professor in Department of Computer Science and Engineering at Chameli Devi group of Institutions, Indore, MP.

Prior to that he has more than 7 years of teaching experience. Now he is pursuing PhD in CSE from RNTU bhooal. He has completed Master of Technology in Computer Science and Engineering, also done Bachelor of Engineering in Computer Science and Engineering. His research includes Computer Network, Network Security, and Machine Learning. He is having various research publications in reputed Scopus, international and national journal, International- National conferences.

AUTHOR - 2

Author-3

Rahul Sharma

Assistant Professor, Computer Science and Engineering, Parul Institute of Technology, Parul University, Vadodara, Gujarat, India

Rahul Sharma is working as an Assistant Professor in the Department of Computer Science and Engineering at Parul Institute of Technology, Parul University, Vadodara, Gujarat. Prior to that, he had more than 5 years of teaching experience in several engineering colleges as Chameli Devi Group of Institutions, Indore, and Dr. A.P.J. Abdul Kalam University. He completed his BTech (CSE) from Patel College of Science and Technology, Indore (M.P.), and MTech

(NM&IS) from SCSIT, DAVV, Indore (M.P.). He is now pursuing PhD degree in Computer Science and Engineering from Rabindranath Tagore University Bhopal (M.P.). His research includes Computer networks, Network Security, Cryptography, and Data Mining. He has 13 research publications in reputed international journals, international–national conferences, and 6 patents (2 published – 4 registered). He also qualified for GATE (CSE) in 2015. He is publishing more than 10+ books in the field of Computer Science and Engineering.

Printed by Libri Plureos GmbH in Hamburg, Germany